CELEBRATING COOKIES

Everyone loves fresh-baked cookies, and this book celebrates all the pleasures of 75 irresistible recipes. You'll find traditional favorites, as well as kid-pleasing goodies, healthy choices, sophisticated tastes, and scrumptious creations for special occasions. The holiday collection offers festive flavors for Christmas and every season of the year. Whether you need a quick snack or something sensational for guests, just reach for this cookbook to find the perfect ooey, gooey, crispy, crunchy indulgence.

LEISURE ARTS
Little Rock, Arkansas

EDITORIAL STAFF

Editor-in-Chief Susan White Sullivan
Designer Relations Director Debra Nettles
Special Projects Director Susan Frantz Wiles
Craft Publications Director Cheryl Johnson
Foods Editor Jane Kenner Prather
Contributing Test Kitchen Staff Rose Glass Klein
Senior Prepress Director Mark Hawkins
Art Publications Director Rhonda Shelby
Contributing Artists Horizon Designs, LLC
Art Category Manager Lora Puls
Graphic Artists Jacob Casleton, Angela Stark, and Janie Wright
Imaging Technicians Stephanie Johnson and Mark R. Potter
Photography Director Katherine Laughlin
Contributing Photographer Mark Mathews
Contributing Photo Stylist Christy Myers
Publishing Systems Administrator Becky Riddle
Publishing Systems Assistants Clint Hanson, John Rose, and Keiji Yumoto

BUSINESS STAFF

Vice President and Chief Operations Officer Tom Siebenmorgen
Director of Finance and Administration Laticia Mull Dittrich
Vice President, Sales and Marketing Pam Stebbins
Sales Director Martha Adams
Marketing Director Margaret Reinold
Creative Services Director Jeff Curtis
Information Technology Director Hermine Linz
Controller Francis Caple
Vice President, Operations Jim Dittrich
Comptroller, Operations Rob Thieme
Retail Customer Service Manager Stan Raynor
Print Production Manager Fred F. Pruss

Library of Congress Control Number: 2009930564
ISBN-13: 978-1-60140-551-7
ISBN-10: 1-60140-551-0

contents

SUCCESS WITH COOKIES

You can be most successful at baking cookies when you know
a few tips from the pros. Here are some of our favorites.

BAKING TIPS

- To keep dough from sticking to cookie cutters, dip in flour before cutting out each cookie. Metal cookie cutters with a good edge usually will cut better than plastic cutters.
- When you need to drizzle a small amount of icing or melted chocolate and you do not have a pastry or decorating bag, use a resealable plastic bag. After filling bag half full of icing or chocolate, seal the bag and cut off a small tip of one corner. Make your first snip small, as you can always cut off more if needed.
- When softening butter in the microwave, be careful not to let it melt, as melted butter results in a flatter cookie.
- Bake one batch of cookies at a time on the center rack of a preheated oven. If baking two batches at a time, space evenly for good air circulation.
- Oven temperatures vary, so always check cookies 1 minute before the earliest time stated in recipe to prevent overbaking.

SUPPLIES

- Use heavy-gauge, shiny aluminum sheets with low or no sides for even browning of cookies. Dark coating on sheets will affect browning. Insulated sheets may make it more difficult to determine doneness; also, cookies with a high butter content will spread out before the shape is set.
- Using parchment paper eliminates the need to grease cookie sheets and makes cleanup easy.

STORAGE TIPS

- After completely cooling cookies, store each kind separately to prevent flavors from blending. Soft cookies will cause crisp cookies to become soft.
- Store soft cookies in an airtight container. Use waxed paper between layers to prevent cookies from sticking together.
- Store crisp cookies in a tin or container with a loose-fitting lid. In humid areas, the lid will need to be tighter so cookies will stay crisp.
- Store bar cookies in the pan covered with foil or remove from pan and store in an airtight container.
- If soft cookies have dried out, place a slice of apple or bread with cookies for a few days in an airtight container.
- Most cookies (except meringues) can be frozen up to six months. Freeze in plastic freezer bags or plastic containers with tight-fitting lids.

MAILING TIPS

- Soft, moist cookies and bar cookies are suitable for mailing. Line a sturdy box with waxed paper, aluminum foil, or plastic wrap. Place a layer of crumpled waxed paper or paper towels in bottom of box. Depending on type of cookie, wrap back-to-back if they are flat, in small groups in plastic bags, or individually.
- Pack crumpled waxed paper or paper towels snugly between cookies to prevent them from shifting. Tape box securely closed.

FAVORITES

Oldies but goodies that you grew up loving—these are the cookies you call your favorites! There's chocolate chip, of course, but also peanut butter, oatmeal, shortbread, sugar cookies, and more. Just one bite can make all your cares melt away. No matter how many new recipes you try, these are the cookies that you want, time after time. They're simply irresistible!

Loaded with creamy chocolate chips, chunky pecans, and ground oats, these rich and chewy cookies are Number One with most Americans.

favorite chocolate chip cookies

In a large bowl, cream butter, sugars, eggs, and vanilla until fluffy. In a separate bowl, combine flour, baking soda, and salt. Add to creamed mixture, mixing thoroughly.

Place oats in a blender or food processor and process until the texture of coarse meal. Stir oats into dough with chocolate chips and pecans. Cover and freeze 1 hour.

Shape dough into 1-inch balls and place on ungreased baking sheets. Bake at 375° for 9 to 12 minutes or until lightly browned around the edges. Cool cookies slightly on baking sheets; transfer to wire racks to cool.

YIELD: about 6 dozen cookies

- 1 cup butter or margarine, softened
- 1 cup granulated sugar
- 1 cup firmly packed brown sugar
- 2 eggs
- 1 teaspoon vanilla extract
- 2 cups all-purpose flour
- 1 teaspoon baking soda
- ½ teaspoon salt
- 2 cups old-fashioned oats
- 1 cup semisweet chocolate chips
- 1 cup chopped pecans

The traditional crisscross pattern alone is enough to identify this crisp favorite! But there's also that wonderful aroma and those delicious little bits of peanuts. Don't forget the milk!

peanut butter cookies

In a large bowl, cream butter and sugars until fluffy. Add peanut butter, egg, and vanilla; beat until well blended. In a small bowl, combine flour, baking soda, baking powder, and salt. Add dry ingredients to creamed mixture; stir until a soft dough forms.

Shape dough into balls slightly larger than 1 inch and place 2 inches apart on ungreased baking sheets. Flatten balls in a crisscross pattern with a fork dipped in flour. Bake at 375° for 6 to 8 minutes or until bottoms are lightly browned. Transfer cookies to wire racks to cool.

YIELD: about 4 dozen cookies

$1/2$ cup butter or margarine, softened

$1/2$ cup granulated sugar

$1/2$ cup firmly packed brown sugar

$3/4$ cup crunchy peanut butter

1 egg

$1/2$ teaspoon vanilla extract

$1 1/3$ cups all-purpose flour

$1/2$ teaspoon baking soda

$1/2$ teaspoon baking powder

$1/4$ teaspoon salt

What a classic! These dense, mild cookies are perfect plain, but don't be afraid to add icing, sugar sprinkles, and other edible decorations. Extra vanilla enriches their flavor.

mom's sugar cookies

In a large bowl, beat oil, eggs, and vanilla until well blended. Add 1 cup sugar; beat until smooth. In a small bowl, combine flour, baking powder, and salt. Add dry ingredients to egg mixture; stir until a soft dough forms.

Drop teaspoonfuls of dough 2 inches apart onto ungreased baking sheets. Flatten cookies with bottom of a glass dipped in sugar. Bake at 400° for 5 to 7 minutes or until bottoms are lightly browned. Transfer cookies to wire racks to cool.

YIELD: about 5 dozen cookies

$3/4$ cup vegetable oil
2 eggs
2 teaspoons vanilla extract
1 cup sugar
2 cups all-purpose flour
1 teaspoon baking powder
$1/4$ teaspoon salt
Sugar

The oatmeal cookie forming the center of our whimsical flower is every bit as good as you remember from childhood. The pretty petals are little golden-edged Lemon Wafers that melt in your mouth.

oatmeal family favorites

In a large bowl, combine 1 cup granulated sugar, brown sugar, and oil; beat until well blended. Add eggs and vanilla; beat until smooth. In a small bowl, combine flour, baking soda, and salt. Add dry ingredients to sugar mixture; stir until a soft dough forms. Stir in oats and coconut until well blended.

Shape dough into 1-inch balls and roll in remaining $3/4$ cup granulated sugar. Place balls 2 inches apart on greased baking sheets; flatten with bottom of a glass dipped in granulated sugar. Bake at 350° for 8 to 10 minutes or until edges are lightly browned. Cool cookies on baking sheets 3 minutes; transfer to wire racks to cool.

YIELD: about 8 dozen cookies

$1^3/4$ cups granulated sugar, divided

1 cup firmly packed brown sugar

1 cup vegetable oil

3 eggs

1 teaspoon vanilla extract

1 cup all-purpose flour

1 teaspoon baking soda

$1/2$ teaspoon salt

4 cups quick-cooking oats

1 cup sweetened shredded coconut

lemon wafers

In a large bowl, cream butter and sugar until fluffy. Add egg, egg whites, and lemon extract; beat until smooth. Add flour to creamed mixture; stir until a thick batter forms.

Spoon batter into a pastry bag fitted with a large round tip. Pipe heaping teaspoonfuls of batter 3 inches apart onto parchment paper-lined baking sheets. Bake at 375° for 7 to 9 minutes or until edges are lightly browned. Transfer cookies to wire racks to cool.

YIELD: about 7 dozen cookies

1 cup butter or margarine, softened

$3/4$ cup sugar

1 egg

2 egg whites

1 tablespoon lemon extract

1 cup all-purpose flour

The ultimate indulgence, these rich cookies are packed with creamy white chocolate chunks and big bites of macadamia nuts. They are sure to disappear fast!

white chocolate chunk macadamia cookies

Cream butter and sugars until light and fluffy. Beat in eggs and vanilla. In a separate bowl, combine flour, baking soda, and salt; gradually add to creamed mixture. Stir in macadamia nuts and white chocolate.

Drop by heaping teaspoonfuls onto greased baking sheets. Bake at 350° for 10 to 12 minutes. Cool cookies slightly on baking sheets; transfer to wire racks to cool.

YIELD: about 6 dozen cookies

- 1 cup butter or margarine, softened
- 1 cup firmly packed light brown sugar
- $\frac{1}{2}$ cup granulated sugar
- 2 eggs
- 1 teaspoon vanilla extract
- $2\frac{1}{4}$ cups all-purpose flour
- 1 teaspoon baking soda
- 1 teaspoon salt
- 1 cup macadamia nuts, coarsely chopped
- 2 cups white baking chocolate, coarsely chopped

Buttery soft and crumbly, our Scottish Shortbread is baked in traditional circles and cut into triangular wedges. The decorative edges are simple to create with a fork.

scottish shortbread

In a large bowl, cream butter and sugars until fluffy. Gradually add flour and stir just until well blended (do not overmix). Shape dough into 2 balls. Press each ball of dough into a 7$\frac{1}{2}$-inch diameter circle onto parchment paper-lined baking sheets. Using a fork, press edges of dough and prick tops several times.

Bake at 325° for 23 to 25 minutes or until edges are lightly browned. Transfer baking sheets to wire racks to cool 10 minutes. Leaving shortbreads on parchment paper, remove paper to a hard cutting surface. Cut each warm shortbread round into 8 wedges; cool.

YIELD: 16 shortbread wedges

1 cup butter, softened

$\frac{1}{4}$ cup plus 2 tablespoons confectioners sugar

$\frac{1}{4}$ cup firmly packed brown sugar

2 cups all-purpose flour

Three forms of chocolate give these cookies a triple dose of flavor. The chocolate chips and chopped walnuts are stirred into the dough right before baking.

chocolate addictions

In a small bowl, beat eggs, sugar, and vanilla until smooth. Stir in baking chocolates and butter. In a small bowl, combine flour and baking powder. Add dry ingredients to creamed mixture; stir until a soft dough forms. Stir in walnuts and chocolate chips.

Drop teaspoonfuls of dough 2 inches apart onto parchment paper-lined baking sheets. Bake at 350° for 7 to 8 minutes or until lightly browned on bottom. Leaving cookies on parchment paper, remove paper from pan. Cool cookies 5 minutes; transfer to wire racks to cool.

YIELD: about 7 dozen cookies

3 eggs
³/₄ cup sugar
1 teaspoon vanilla extract
4 ounces semisweet baking chocolate, melted
4 ounces unsweetened baking chocolate, melted
3 tablespoons unsalted butter or margarine, melted
¹/₃ cup all-purpose flour
¹/₄ teaspoon baking powder
1¹/₂ cups coarsely chopped walnuts
1 cup semisweet chocolate chips

With a name that makes you giggle, Snickerdoodles have timeless appeal. These sweet treats can be made up in a jiffy with ingredients kept on hand in most pantries. Their pretty look comes from rolling the balls of dough in a cinnamon-sugar mixture before baking.

snickerdoodles

In a large bowl, cream butter and 1$\frac{1}{4}$ cups sugar until fluffy. Add eggs and vanilla; beat until smooth. In a medium bowl, combine flour, $\frac{1}{2}$ teaspoon cinnamon, cream of tartar, baking soda, and salt. Add dry ingredients to creamed mixture; stir until a soft dough forms. In a small bowl, combine remaining $\frac{1}{4}$ cup sugar and 1 teaspoon cinnamon.

Shape dough into 1-inch balls and roll in sugar mixture. Place balls 2 inches apart on lightly greased baking sheets. Bake at 375° for 6 to 8 minutes or until bottoms are lightly browned. Transfer cookies to wire racks to cool.

YIELD: about 7 dozen cookies

- 1 cup butter or margarine, softened
- 1$\frac{1}{2}$ cups sugar, divided
- 2 eggs
- 1 teaspoon vanilla extract
- 2$\frac{1}{2}$ cups all-purpose flour
- 1$\frac{1}{2}$ teaspoons ground cinnamon, divided
- 1 teaspoon cream of tartar
- 1 teaspoon baking soda
- $\frac{1}{4}$ teaspoon salt

Thin and chewy, these little favorites have a spicy kick. No wonder they've held their own for so long on the list of favorites!

old-fashioned gingersnaps

In a large bowl, cream butter and 2 cups sugar until fluffy. Add eggs and molasses; beat until smooth. In a medium bowl, combine flour, baking soda, cinnamon, cloves, and ginger. Add dry ingredients to creamed mixture; stir until a soft dough forms.

Shape dough into 1-inch balls and roll in remaining $3/4$ cup sugar. Place balls 3 inches apart on lightly greased baking sheets; flatten with bottom of a glass dipped in sugar. Bake at 375° for 5 to 7 minutes or until bottoms are lightly browned. Transfer cookies to wire racks to cool.

YIELD: about 10 dozen cookies

1½ cups butter or margarine, softened

2¾ cups sugar, divided

2 eggs

½ cup molasses

4 cups all-purpose flour

2 teaspoons baking soda

2 teaspoons ground cinnamon

2 teaspoons ground cloves

2 teaspoons ground ginger

These tender, mild cutouts really stack up high scores with cookie lovers. Their comforting taste and texture is oh, so good!

sandies

In a large bowl, cream butter and sugars until fluffy. Add egg and vanilla; beat until smooth. In a medium bowl, combine flour, pecans, and salt. Add dry ingredients to creamed mixture; stir until a soft dough forms. Divide dough in half; wrap in plastic wrap and chill 1 hour.

On a lightly floured surface, roll out half of dough at a time to $1/4$-inch thickness. Use a $2^1/2$-inch round fluted-edge cookie cutter to cut out cookies. Transfer to ungreased baking sheets. Bake at 350° for 7 to 9 minutes or until bottoms are lightly browned. Transfer cookies to wire racks to cool.

YIELD: about $2^1/2$ dozen cookies

- $3/4$ cup butter or margarine, softened
- $3/4$ cup confectioners sugar
- $1/4$ cup firmly packed brown sugar
- 1 egg
- $1^1/2$ teaspoons vanilla extract
- $2^1/4$ cups all-purpose flour
- $1/2$ cup chopped pecans, toasted and finely ground
- $1/4$ teaspoon salt

Get ready to dig in to goodness! Crisp rice cereal enhances these light bites of nutty delight. The dough is shaped into a roll and refrigerated before slicing and baking.

pecan crispies

In a large bowl, cream butter and sugars until fluffy. Add eggs and vanilla-butter-nut flavoring; beat until smooth. In a small bowl, combine flour, baking soda, and baking powder. Add dry ingredients to creamed mixture. Stir in oats, cereal, and pecans. Shape dough into four 8-inch-long rolls. Wrap in plastic wrap and chill 2 hours.

Cut dough into 1/4-inch-thick slices. Place 2 inches apart on greased baking sheets. Bake at 325° for 8 to 10 minutes or until bottoms are lightly browned. Transfer cookies to wire racks to cool.

YIELD: about 8 dozen cookies

- 1 cup butter or margarine, softened
- 1 cup firmly packed brown sugar
- 1 cup granulated sugar
- 2 eggs
- 1 teaspoon vanilla-butter-nut flavoring
- 1½ cups all-purpose flour
- ½ teaspoon baking soda
- ½ teaspoon baking powder
- 2 cups quick-cooking oats
- 1½ cups crispy rice cereal
- 1 cup finely chopped pecans, toasted

SPECIAL OCCASIONS

When the celebration calls for treats as special as the occasion, creative cookies are the answer. This sampling offers something sweet for many of life's milestones, including weddings, birthdays, and even graduation day! Whatever the reason, make the day extra memorable with these delectable delights.

Sweet lemon sandwich cookies make perfectly delicious wedding favors, and you won't believe how easy it is to make them! Simply spread buttery crackers with store-bought lemon frosting, dip them in melted candy coating, and pipe on the newlyweds' monogram.

monogrammed cookies

Place half of crackers (about 75 crackers) upside-down on waxed paper. Spoon frosting into a decorating bag fitted with a large round tip. Pipe about 1 teaspoon frosting onto each cracker. Place remaining crackers on top of frosting and press lightly.

In a heavy medium saucepan, melt candy coating and lemon oil over low heat. Remove from heat. Place each cracker sandwich on a fork and dip into candy coating until covered. Place on waxed paper and allow candy coating to harden.

For monogram, tint decorating icing desired color. Spoon icing into a decorating bag fitted with a #2 round tip. Pipe monogram on each cookie; allow to harden.

YIELD: about 6 dozen sandwich cookies

1½ **packages (12 ounces each) butter-flavored crackers**

1 **can (16 ounces) lemon-flavored ready-to-spread frosting**

2 **pounds, 10 ounces vanilla candy coating**

¼ **teaspoon lemon-flavored oil (used in candy making)**

1 **container (16 ounces) white decorating icing (used in cake decorating)**

Desired color of paste food coloring for monogram

Ring-shaped cookies in graduated sizes are stacked to create this pretty centerpiece for a bridal shower. We embellished the beautiful confection with tiny sugared violas, loops of icing, and a big ribbon bow.

almond cookie tree

For cookies, use a black pen to draw 13 circles on sheets of parchment paper, 3 inches apart, beginning with a 1-inch-diameter circle. Increase the size of each circle by $1/2$ inch, ending with a 7-inch-diameter circle. Place almond paste in a large microwave-safe bowl. Microwave on high power (100%) 25 seconds to soften. Add butter and beat with an electric mixer until smooth. Add confectioners sugar and beat until fluffy. Add eggs and extracts; beat until smooth. In a small bowl, combine flour and cornstarch. Gradually add dry ingredients to creamed mixture; stir until a very soft dough forms.

Spoon dough into a decorating bag fitted with a very large round tip (#1A). Turn parchment paper over, with lines facing down, on a baking sheet and pipe dough around outside edges of circles. To reinforce each of the 3 largest circles, pipe a second circle of dough just inside and touching first dough circle. Bake at 350° for 12 to 14 minutes or until bottoms are lightly browned. Transfer cookies to wire racks with waxed paper underneath to cool.

For sugared violas, combine water and meringue powder; brush violas with mixture and coat with superfine sugar. Allow to dry.

For icing, combine all ingredients in a small bowl; stir until smooth. Spoon icing into a decorating bag fitted with a small round tip. Pipe loops of icing onto each cookie. Allow icing to harden. To stack cookies, pipe a ring of icing onto a serving plate and place largest cookie on icing. Stack remaining cookies from largest to smallest. Use a small amount of icing to adhere sugared violas to cookies.

YIELD: one 7 $1/2$-inch-high cookie tree

COOKIES

- 1 can (8 ounces) almond paste, coarsely crumbled
- 1 cup butter or margarine, softened
- $1 1/4$ cups confectioners sugar
- 2 eggs
- 1 teaspoon almond extract
- $1/2$ teaspoon vanilla extract
- 2 cups all-purpose flour
- $3/4$ cup cornstarch

SUGARED VIOLAS

- 2 tablespoons water
- 2 teaspoons meringue powder
- 16 to 18 fresh viola flowers
  Superfine sugar

ICING

- 1 cup confectioners sugar
- $4 1/2$ teaspoons milk
- $1/8$ teaspoon almond extract

Served in a brand-new tool box, these rich cookies are enticing refreshments for a groom's shower. Be sure you share the recipes so the bride can make more later as sweet encouragements for doing household chores. Honey-Do Bars are chewy blond brownies flavored with brown sugar and honey. Rolled in chocolaty cookie crumbs, rewarding Mocha-Nut Balls combine toasted pecans and coffee-flavored liqueur.

honey-do bars

In a large bowl, cream butter and brown sugar until fluffy. Add honey, egg, and vanilla; beat until smooth. In a small bowl, combine dry ingredients. Add to creamed mixture; stir until well blended. Stir in pecans. Spread batter into a lightly greased 9 x 13-inch baking pan.

Bake at 350° for 28 to 30 minutes or until mixture starts to pull away from sides of pan. Cool in pan 15 minutes. Cut into 2-inch squares while warm; cool completely in pan.

YIELD: about 2 dozen bars

- $1/2$ cup butter or margarine, softened
- $1^1/2$ cups firmly packed brown sugar
- $1/3$ cup honey
- 1 egg
- 1 teaspoon vanilla extract
- $1^3/4$ cups all-purpose flour
- $1^1/2$ teaspoons baking powder
- $1/2$ teaspoon baking soda
- $1/4$ teaspoon salt
- 1 cup chopped pecans, toasted

mocha-nut balls

Process cookies in a food processor until finely ground. In a large bowl, combine $2^3/4$ cups cookie crumbs, pecans, and confectioners sugar. Stir in liqueur, corn syrup, and vanilla. Shape mixture into 1-inch balls; roll in remaining cookie crumbs. Store in refrigerator.

YIELD: about $4^1/2$ dozen cookies

- 34 chocolate sandwich cookies
- $1^1/2$ cups chopped pecans, toasted and coarsely ground
- 1 cup confectioners sugar
- $1/3$ cup coffee-flavored liqueur or coffee
- $1/4$ cup light corn syrup
- 1 tablespoon vanilla extract

Kissed with honey and a touch of cinnamon, our Peanut Butter Bears make adorable snacks for a baby shower. Color their bow ties to reflect whether a girl or boy is expected, or use both pink and blue when the gender is still a secret.

peanut butter bears

In a large bowl, cream butter, peanut butter, and sugars; beat until fluffy. Add eggs and honey; beat until smooth. In a medium bowl, combine flour, cinnamon, baking soda, baking powder, and salt. Add dry ingredients to creamed mixture; stir until a soft dough forms. Divide dough into fourths.

On a lightly floured surface, roll out one fourth of dough at a time to $1/8$-inch thickness. Use a $3^1/2$ x 4-inch bear-shaped cookie cutter to cut out cookies. Place 1 inch apart on greased baking sheets. Press chocolate chips, flat side up, into cookies for eyes and noses.

Bake at 350° for 7 to 10 minutes or until bottoms are lightly browned. Cool cookies on baking sheets for 2 minutes; transfer to wire racks to cool completely. Transfer chocolate icing into a decorating bag fitted with a very small round tip. Pipe ears and mouth onto each bear. Transfer pink or blue icing into a decorating bag fitted with a small round tip. Pipe ribbon onto each bear. Allow icing to harden.

YIELD: about 3 dozen cookies

$3/4$ cup butter or margarine, softened

1 cup smooth peanut butter

1 cup firmly packed brown sugar

$3/4$ cup granulated sugar

2 eggs

2 tablespoons honey

$2^1/2$ cups all-purpose flour

$1/2$ teaspoon ground cinnamon

$1/2$ teaspoon baking soda

$1/2$ teaspoon baking powder

$1/4$ teaspoon salt

Semisweet chocolate mini chips

1 tube (4.25 ounces) chocolate decorating icing

1 tube (4.25 ounces) pink and/or blue decorating icing

A good choice for a toddler's party, this simple recipe is fun to make in different shapes. Our dinosaurs and flowers are just two examples of the many variations possible.

flower or dinosaur cinnamon cookies

Cream butter and sugars in a large bowl until fluffy. Add eggs, milk, and vanilla; beat until smooth. In a medium bowl, combine flour, cinnamon, baking powder, baking soda, and salt. Add dry ingredients to creamed mixture; stir until a soft dough forms. Tint desired color. Divide dough into fourths. Wrap in plastic wrap and chill 3 hours or until firm enough to handle.

On a lightly floured surface, roll out one fourth of dough at a time to $1/4$-inch thickness. Use a 4-inch diameter flower-shaped or a $6^1/_2$ x $2^1/_2$-inch dinosaur-shaped cookie cutter to cut out cookies. Place 2 inches apart on lightly greased baking sheets. Sprinkle center of each flower with white sparkling sugar or sprinkle each dinosaur with multi-colored non-pareils, lightly pressing into dough.

Bake at 375° for 6 to 8 minutes or until edges are lightly browned. Transfer cookies to wire racks to cool.

YIELD: about 20 flower or dinosaur cookies

1 cup butter or margarine, softened

$1^1/_2$ cups granulated sugar

$^1/_2$ cup firmly packed brown sugar

4 eggs

$1^1/_2$ tablespoons milk

$1^1/_2$ teaspoons vanilla extract

$4^1/_4$ cups all-purpose flour

$1^1/_2$ teaspoons ground cinnamon

$^3/_4$ teaspoon baking powder

$^1/_2$ teaspoon baking soda

$^1/_2$ teaspoon salt

For flowers: rose paste food coloring and white sparkling sugar

For dinosaurs: violet paste food coloring and multi-colored non-pareils

This giant cookie "lollipop" lets you say "Happy Birthday" in a big way. For the presentation, wrap it in cellophane and tie off with a colorful ribbon and tag.

happy birthday cookie

For cookie, cream butter and sugars in a medium bowl until fluffy. Add egg, oil, and vanilla; beat until smooth. In a small bowl, combine flour, baking soda, and salt. Add dry ingredients to creamed mixture; stir until a soft dough forms. Stir in $1/3$ cup candies, oats, and cereal. Press dough into a greased 12-inch-diameter pizza pan. Sprinkle remaining $1/3$ cup candies on top of dough. Bake at 325° for 23 to 25 minutes or until top is lightly browned. Transfer pan to a wire rack to cool completely.

For icing, combine confectioners sugar, cocoa, milk, and vanilla in a small bowl; stir until smooth. Transfer cooled cookie to a 12-inch-diameter cardboard cake board with a 20-inch wooden $3/8$-inch-diameter dowel rod glued to the back. Drizzle icing over cookie; let icing harden.

YIELD: about 12 servings

COOKIE

- $1/3$ cup butter or margarine, softened
- $1/3$ cup granulated sugar
- $1/3$ cup firmly packed brown sugar
- 1 egg
- $1/4$ cup vegetable oil
- 1 teaspoon vanilla extract
- 1 cup plus 3 tablespoons all-purpose flour
- $1/2$ teaspoon baking soda
- $1/4$ teaspoon salt
- $2/3$ cup candy-coated chocolate mini baking candies, divided
- $1/3$ cup quick-cooking oats
- $1/3$ cup crispy rice cereal

ICING

- $1/2$ cup confectioners sugar
- 2 teaspoons cocoa
- 3 to 4 teaspoons milk
- $1/2$ teaspoon vanilla extract

A child's party calls for cookies and ice cream, and this recipe is a real kid-pleaser! The treats are shaped and iced to resemble ice-cream cones, with bubble gum flavoring for an extra surprise.

ice-cream cone cookies

For cookies, place almond paste in a large microwave-safe bowl. Microwave on high power (100%) 25 seconds to soften. Add butter and sugars to almond paste; cream until fluffy. Add egg, vanilla, and flavored oil; beat until smooth. Gradually add flour; stir until a soft dough forms. Divide dough into thirds. Wrap in plastic wrap and chill 1 hour.

On a lightly floured surface, roll out one third of dough at a time to $1/4$-inch thickness. Use a $2^1/2$ x $3^3/4$-inch ice-cream cone-shaped cookie cutter to cut out cookies. Transfer to lightly greased baking sheets. Bake at 350° for 7 to 9 minutes or until bottoms are lightly browned. Transfer cookies to wire racks with waxed paper underneath to cool.

For icing, combine confectioners sugar, milk, and flavored oil in a medium bowl; stir until smooth. Tint pink. Ice tops of cookies to resemble ice cream; sprinkle with confetti sprinkles before icing hardens. Allow icing to harden.

YIELD: about 4 dozen cookies

COOKIES

- 1 can (8 ounces) almond paste, coarsely crumbled
- $3/4$ cup butter or margarine, softened
- $1/2$ cup granulated sugar
- $1/2$ cup confectioners sugar
- 1 egg
- $1/2$ teaspoon vanilla extract
- $1/8$ teaspoon bubble gum-flavored oil (used in candy making)
- $2^1/4$ cups all-purpose flour

ICING

- 2 cups confectioners sugar
- 3 tablespoons milk
- 10 drops bubble gum-flavored oil (used in candy making)

  Pink paste food coloring

  Pastel confetti sprinkles

Rambunctious boys will go wild over these cookies, which are right on track for an adventurous party at the zoo or in your own backyard. Brown jelly beans and chocolate sprinkles make the claws truly awesome!

paw print cookies

For cookies, cream butter, brown sugar, and extracts in a medium bowl until fluffy. Add flour; stir until a soft dough forms. Stir in cereal. Shape dough into 2-inch balls and place 3 inches apart on greased baking sheets. Press into irregularly shaped 3-inch-diameter cookies. Press 4 jelly beans into each cookie for toe pads. Press chocolate sprinkles above toe pads for claws.

Bake at 325° for 14 to 16 minutes or until bottoms are lightly browned. Cool on baking sheets 5 minutes. Using a large spatula, carefully transfer cookies to wire racks to cool completely.

For icing, combine confectioners sugar, chocolate syrup, and milk; stir until smooth. Spoon icing on each cookie for paw pad. Allow icing to harden.

YIELD: about 1 dozen cookies

COOKIES

- 1^{1}/$_{4}$ cups butter or margarine, softened
- ^{1}/$_{2}$ cup firmly packed brown sugar
- ^{3}/$_{4}$ teaspoon vanilla extract
- ^{3}/$_{4}$ teaspoon orange extract
- 2^{1}/$_{2}$ cups all-purpose flour
- ^{3}/$_{4}$ cup crushed corn flake cereal
- Brown gourmet jelly beans
- Chocolate sprinkles

ICING

- 1^{1}/$_{4}$ cups confectioners sugar
- 2 tablespoons chocolate syrup
- 1 tablespoon milk

Pamper your little sweetheart with a dress-up party where everyone gets her own tasty necklace. The decorated cookies have two heart-shaped cutouts—one to fill with a melted candy "jewel" and the other for threading the ribbon necklace.

tasty necklace cookies

For cookies, cream butter and sugar in a medium bowl until fluffy. Add egg and extracts; beat until smooth. In a small bowl, combine flour, baking powder, and salt. Add dry ingredients to creamed mixture; stir until a soft dough forms. Divide dough into fourths. Wrap in plastic wrap and chill 1 to 2 hours.

On a lightly floured surface, roll out one fourth of dough at a time to $1/8$-inch thickness. Use a 3-inch-wide scalloped-edge heart-shaped cookie cutter to cut out cookies. Place 2 inches apart on lightly greased foil-lined baking sheets. Use a miniature heart-shaped cookie cutter to cut out heart in center of each cookie. Use a heart-shaped aspic cutter to cut out hole in top center of each cookie for ribbon. Lightly press non-pareils into cookies. Bake at 400° for 6 to 8 minutes or until edges are lightly browned. Allow cookies to cool slightly. Leaving cookies on foil, remove foil from pan; cool completely.

For candy, combine sugar, water, corn syrup, vinegar, and salt in a heavy small saucepan. Stirring constantly, cook over medium heat until sugar dissolves. Using a pastry brush dipped in hot water, wash down any sugar crystals on sides of pan. Attach a candy thermometer to pan, making sure thermometer does not touch bottom of pan. Increase heat to medium-high and bring to a boil. Cook syrup, without stirring, until it reaches soft-crack stage (approximately 270° to 290°). Test about $1/2$ teaspoon syrup in ice water. Syrup will form hard thread in ice water but will soften when removed from the water. Remove from heat; tint pink. Spoon about $1/2$ teaspoonful candy into large cutout of each cookie. If necessary, reheat candy on low heat if it becomes too firm. Cool until candy hardens; remove cookies from foil. Thread a 24-inch length of ribbon through small heart in each cookie to make necklace.

YIELD: about $3^1/2$ dozen cookies

COOKIES

- $1/2$ cup butter or margarine, softened
- 1 cup sugar
- 1 egg
- 1 teaspoon vanilla extract
- $1/4$ teaspoon almond extract
- 2 cups all-purpose flour
- 2 teaspoons baking powder
- $1/2$ teaspoon salt
  Pink and white non-pareils

CANDY

- $2/3$ cup sugar
- $1/2$ cup water
- 2 tablespoons light corn syrup
- $1/2$ teaspoon white vinegar
- $1/8$ teaspoon salt
  Pink paste food coloring
  Ribbon

Fresh apples and a supply of sharpened pencils will win any teacher's heart—especially when the gifts are actually delicious cookies! Our Marzipan Apple Cookies cleverly feature clove stems and gumdrop leaves. The "pencils" are flavorful Hazelnut Cookies with lots of yummy icing.

hazelnut cookies

For cookies, cream butter and sugar in a medium bowl until fluffy. Add egg and vanilla; beat until smooth. Stir in hazelnuts. Add flour and salt; stir until a soft dough forms. On a lightly floured surface, roll out dough to a 12-inch square. Cut out 1 x 6-inch cookies, cutting one end of each cookie into a point. Transfer to greased baking sheets. Bake at 350° for 7 to 11 minutes or until edges are lightly browned. Transfer cookies to wire racks to cool.

For icing, combine confectioners sugar and milk in a medium bowl; stir until smooth. Transfer $1/4$ cup icing to each of 3 small bowls; tint brown, pink, and black. Tint remaining icing yellow. Refer to photo and ice cookies, allowing icing to harden between each color.

YIELD: about $2^1/2$ dozen cookies

COOKIES
- $3/4$ cup butter or margarine, softened
- $2/3$ cup sugar
- 1 egg
- 1 teaspoon vanilla extract
- $2/3$ cup finely ground hazelnuts
- $2^1/4$ cups all-purpose flour
- $1/4$ teaspoon salt

ICING
- 4 cups confectioners sugar
- $1/2$ cup plus 1 tablespoon milk
- Brown, pink, black, and yellow paste food coloring

marzipan apple cookies

Place almond paste in a large microwave-safe bowl. Microwave on high power (100%) 25 seconds to soften. Add butter and beat with an electric mixer until smooth. Add sugar and beat until fluffy. Add egg and vanilla; beat until smooth. Add flour and salt to creamed mixture; stir until a soft dough forms. Tint red. Divide dough in half. Cover dough and chill 1 hour.

Shape heaping teaspoonfuls of dough into about $1^1/4$-inch-diameter balls. Use thumb to make a slight indentation in top of each ball. Insert a whole clove and a small sliver of gumdrop into indentation for stem and leaf. Place dough on parchment-lined baking sheets. Bake at 350° for 9 to 11 minutes or until bottoms are lightly browned. Transfer cookies to wire racks to cool.

YIELD: about 5 dozen cookies

- 1 can (8 ounces) almond paste, coarsely crumbled
- 1 cup butter, softened
- $1/4$ cup sugar
- 1 egg
- 1 teaspoon vanilla extract
- $2^1/2$ cups all-purpose flour
- $1/8$ teaspoon salt
- Red paste food coloring
- Whole cloves (for stems)
- Green gumdrops (for leaves)

A creamy white chocolate filling is piped into rolled wafers for our miniature "diplomas." Tied with ribbons in the graduate's school colors, the treats are a novel way to celebrate scholarly success.

graduation day cookies

In a medium bowl, cream butter and sugar until fluffy. Stir in flour. In a small bowl, beat egg whites until foamy. Beat egg whites and almond extract into dough. Making 4 to 6 cookies at a time, drop teaspoonfuls of dough 4 inches apart onto parchment paper-lined baking sheets. Spread dough slightly with the back of a spoon.

Bake at 400° for 5 to 6 minutes or until edges are lightly browned. Roll each warm cookie around handle of a small wooden spoon. Transfer cookies to wire racks, seam side down, to cool.

Stirring constantly, melt chocolate over low heat in a small saucepan. Remove from heat. Stir in shortening; allow mixture to cool slightly. Spoon chocolate mixture into a decorating bag fitted with a small round tip. Pipe chocolate into cookie rolls; allow chocolate to harden. Tie ribbons around cookies.

YIELD: about 3^1/$_2$ dozen cookies

^{1}/$_2$ cup butter or margarine, softened

^{1}/$_2$ cup sugar

^{1}/$_2$ cup all-purpose flour

2 egg whites

1 teaspoon almond extract

6 ounces white baking chocolate

1 teaspoon vegetable shortening

Narrow ribbons in school colors

KIDS COLLECTION

When you're making cookies for kids, be sure "fun" is one of the ingredients! This collection of recipes makes it easy to choose cookies with a touch of silliness or a taste that tickles their fancy.

Imagine all the fun that kids can have with these creative hamburger look-alikes! But even the grownups will be surprised by how good they taste and how simple they are to make. The "buns" are sugar cookies from slice-and-bake refrigerator dough. The "lettuce" is tinted coconut. And the "burger" is ready-to-spread chocolate frosting.

sugar cookie "burgers"

Cookies are best eaten the day they are made.

Cut cookie dough into ¼-inch-thick slices. Place 2 inches apart on ungreased baking sheets; shape into rounds. On half of cookies, press ½ teaspoon peanuts into each cookie. Bake at 350° for 8 to 10 minutes or until tops are lightly browned. Transfer cookies to wire racks to cool.

Place coconut in a resealable plastic bag. Add 5 to 6 drops food coloring. Shake bag until coconut is evenly tinted; set aside.

Spread 1 tablespoon frosting over flat side of each plain cookie; sprinkle about 1½ tablespoons coconut over frosting. Spread 1 teaspoon frosting over flat side of each peanut cookie. Place peanut cookies on coconut-covered cookies; gently squeeze cookies together.

YIELD: about 16 cookie "burgers"

1 package (18 ounces) refrigerated sugar cookie dough

¼ cup chopped peanuts

1½ cups sweetened flaked coconut

Green liquid food coloring

1 container (16 ounces) chocolate ready-to-spread frosting

Delivery pizza can't beat this one! Chewy, gooey Candy Bar Pizzas are chock-full of peanuts, chocolate, and caramel. The oatmeal crust, featuring brown sugar and chunky peanut butter, is a tasty sweet all by itself!

candy bar pizzas

For crust, combine oats, brown sugar, and corn syrup in a large bowl. Add melted butter, peanut butter, and vanilla; stir until well blended. Press mixture into bottoms of two 9-inch round cake pans. Bake at 350° for 10 to 12 minutes or until lightly browned. Cool in pans 10 minutes.

For filling, microwave caramels and water in a medium microwave-safe bowl on high power (100%) 2 minutes, stirring after 1 minute. Spread evenly over crusts. Microwave chocolate chips in a medium microwave-safe bowl on medium-high power (80%) 2 minutes, stirring after 1 minute. Add peanut butter and shortening; stir until well blended. Stir in peanuts.

Spread filling over caramel layers. Chill 30 minutes or until chocolate is firm. Cut into wedges to serve.

YIELD: two 9-inch pizzas, 16 servings each

CRUST

- 2 cups quick-cooking oats
- 1/2 cup firmly packed brown sugar
- 1/3 cup light corn syrup
- 2 tablespoons butter or margarine, melted
- 2 tablespoons chunky peanut butter
- 1/2 teaspoon vanilla extract

FILLING

- 26 caramels (about 1/2 of a 14-ounce package)
- 2 tablespoons water
- 1 package (6 ounces) semisweet chocolate chips
- 1/3 cup chunky peanut butter
- 2 teaspoons vegetable shortening
- 1/2 cup salted peanuts

Rustle up these yummy treats any time the kids are poking around for a snack. Cowboy Cookies corral three childhood favorites—chewy oats, chocolate chips, and pecans—in one tasty morsel!

cowboy cookies

In a large bowl, beat butter and sugars until creamy. Add eggs and vanilla; beat until smooth. In a small bowl, combine flour, baking powder, baking soda, and salt. Add dry ingredients to creamed mixture; stir until a soft dough forms. Stir in oats, chocolate chips, and pecans.

Drop tablespoonfuls of dough 2 inches apart onto lightly greased baking sheets. Bake at 350° for 9 to 11 minutes or until edges are lightly browned. Transfer cookies to wire racks to cool.

YIELD: about $5\frac{1}{2}$ dozen cookies

1 cup butter or margarine, melted

1 cup granulated sugar

1 cup firmly packed brown sugar

2 eggs

1 teaspoon vanilla extract

2 cups all-purpose flour

1 teaspoon baking powder

1 teaspoon baking soda

$\frac{1}{2}$ teaspoon salt

2 cups quick-cooking oats

1 package (12 ounces) semisweet chocolate chips

$\frac{3}{4}$ cup chopped pecans

The next time your children deserve a gold star for being good, bring out these cookie stars instead! They taste like everyone's favorite sandwich— only better! Peanut butter cookies serve as the "bread," and raspberry jelly sweetens the frosting-like filling.

peanut butter and jelly creams

For cookies, cream butter, peanut butter, sugars, and egg until fluffy. In a small bowl, combine dry ingredients; add to creamed mixture. Stir until a soft dough forms. Cover dough and chill 2 hours.

Divide chilled dough into fourths. On a heavily floured surface, roll out one fourth of dough at a time to $\frac{1}{8}$-inch thickness. Use a 3-inch-wide star-shaped cookie cutter to cut out cookies. Transfer to ungreased baking sheets. Bake at 350° for 7 to 9 minutes or until bottoms are lightly browned. Transfer cookies to wire racks to cool.

For filling, combine first 4 ingredients in a small bowl. Tint pink. Spread about 2 teaspoons of filling between 2 cookies. Repeat with remaining filling and cookies.

YIELD: about 2 dozen cookies

COOKIES

- $\frac{3}{4}$ cup butter or margarine, softened
- $\frac{1}{2}$ cup smooth peanut butter
- $\frac{1}{2}$ cup granulated sugar
- $\frac{1}{2}$ cup firmly packed brown sugar
- 1 egg
- $1\frac{1}{4}$ cups all-purpose flour
- 1 teaspoon baking powder
- $\frac{1}{4}$ teaspoon salt

FILLING

- $1\frac{3}{4}$ cups confectioners sugar
- $\frac{1}{4}$ cup butter or margarine, softened
- 4 teaspoons whipping cream
- 4 teaspoons raspberry jelly
- Pink paste food coloring

...mbination for family game night! Chocolate-Nut Sundae ...me-like cakes full of maraschino cherries and chopped ...g of melted chocolate tops them off. The moist and chewy ...utter Brownies are covered with crunchy peanuts.

chocolate-nut sundae squares

In a large bowl, cream butter and brown sugar until fluffy. Add egg, reserved cherry liquid, and vanilla; beat until smooth. In a small bowl, combine flour, chocolate drink mix, and baking powder. Add dry ingredients to creamed mixture; stir until a soft dough forms. Stir in pecans and cherries. Line a 9-inch square baking pan with aluminum foil, extending foil over opposite sides of pan; grease foil. Spread mixture into prepared pan. Bake at 350° for 20 to 25 minutes or until firm. Cool in pan 10 minutes. Use foil to lift out of pan; cool.

Melt chocolate chips and shortening in a small saucepan over low heat. Drizzle melted chocolate over baked mixture. Cut into 2-inch squares.

YIELD: about 16 squares

- ½ cup butter or margarine, softened
- ⅔ cup firmly packed brown sugar
- 1 egg
- 1 jar (10 ounces) maraschino cherries, drained and chopped, reserving ¼ cup liquid
- ½ teaspoon vanilla extract
- 1½ cups all-purpose flour
- ½ cup chocolate drink mix for milk
- ½ teaspoon baking powder
- 1 cup chopped pecans
- ⅓ cup semisweet chocolate chips
- ½ teaspoon vegetable shortening

nutty peanut butter brownies

In a large bowl, cream peanut butter, butter, and brown sugar until fluffy. Add eggs and vanilla; beat until smooth. In a small bowl, combine flour, baking powder, and salt. Add dry ingredients to creamed mixture; stir until well blended.

Line a 9 x 13-inch baking pan with aluminum foil, extending foil over ends of pan; grease foil. Spread batter in prepared pan; sprinkle peanuts over top. Bake at 375° for 15 to 18 minutes or until edges are lightly browned. Cool in pan 10 minutes. Use foil to lift brownies from pan. Cut warm brownies into 2-inch squares; cool.

YIELD: about 2 dozen brownies

- ¾ cup smooth peanut butter
- ½ cup butter or margarine, softened
- 1½ cups firmly packed brown sugar
- 2 eggs
- 2 teaspoons vanilla extract
- 1½ cups all-purpose flour
- 1½ teaspoons baking powder
- ⅛ teaspoon salt
- ½ cup chopped peanuts

Powdered sugar puts a fun finish on the face of these rich chocolate cookies. The cracked patterns appear naturally as the dough expands during baking. The addition of malted milk crunch makes the cookies taste reminiscent of a soda-fountain favorite.

chocolate malted cookies

Combine sugar, melted chocolate, and melted butter in a large bowl. Add eggs, 1 at a time, beating well after each addition. In a small bowl, combine flour, baking powder, and salt. Add dry ingredients to chocolate mixture; stir until a soft dough forms. Stir in $3/4$ cup malted milk crunch. Cover dough and chill 1 hour.

Shape dough into 1-inch balls. In a small bowl, combine remaining $1/4$ cup malted milk crunch and confectioners sugar. Roll balls in confectioners sugar mixture and place 2 inches apart on parchment paper-lined baking sheets.

Bake at 300° for 10 to 12 minutes or until tops are cracked. Cool cookies on baking sheets 3 minutes; transfer to wire racks to cool.

YIELD: about 6$1/2$ dozen cookies

- 2 cups granulated sugar
- 6 ounces semisweet baking chocolate, melted
- $1/4$ cup butter or margarine, melted
- 4 eggs
- 2 cups all-purpose flour
- 2 teaspoons baking powder
- $1/2$ teaspoon salt
- 1 cup malted milk crunch, divided (used in candy making)
- $3/4$ cup confectioners sugar

Got milk? Kids will definitely want a big glass to go with these delicious cookies. Loaded with butterscotch chips and pecans, Butterscotch Chewies live up to their tempting name.

butterscotch chewies

In a large bowl, cream butter and brown sugar until fluffy. Add eggs and vanilla; beat until smooth. In a medium bowl, combine flour and baking soda. Add dry ingredients to creamed mixture; stir until a soft dough forms. Stir in butterscotch chips and pecans.

Drop tablespoonfuls of dough 2 inches apart onto greased baking sheets. Bake at 375° for 7 to 9 minutes or until bottoms are lightly browned. Transfer cookies to wire racks to cool. Store in single layers between sheets of waxed paper.

YIELD: about 4 dozen cookies

- $^2/_3$ cup butter or margarine, softened
- $1^1/_2$ cups firmly packed brown sugar
- 2 eggs
- 1 teaspoon vanilla extract
- $1^1/_2$ cups all-purpose flour
- $^1/_4$ teaspoon baking soda
- 1 package (10 or 12 ounces) butterscotch chips
- 1 cup chopped pecans

These sweet hearts are perfect for a little girl's tea party. The no-bake treats are extra easy to make using crispy cocoa-flavored rice cereal and peanut butter. For other party themes, mold them in different shapes, or press the mixture into a rectangular baking pan and cut in squares or bars.

no-bake cocoa hearts

In a heavy medium saucepan, combine sugar and corn syrup over medium-high heat; stir frequently until mixture boils. Allow to boil 30 seconds without stirring. Remove from heat and stir in peanut butter. Place cereal in a large bowl. Pour peanut butter mixture over cereal; stir until well blended.

With well-greased hands, press mixture into a greased 3³/₄-inch-wide by 1-inch-deep heart-shaped mold. Immediately remove from mold; transfer to lightly greased aluminum foil to cool. Repeat with remaining cereal, working quickly before mixture cools and greasing mold as necessary. (Mixture may be pressed into a 9 x 13-inch baking pan, if desired.)

YIELD: about 10 hearts

1 cup sugar

1 cup light corn syrup

1 cup smooth peanut butter

6 cups cocoa-flavored crispy rice cereal

Here's a new twist on an old favorite—our Sugared Chocolate Pretzels are made with cocoa and sprinkled with sparkling sugar before baking. Kids will love helping roll the dough into ropes and twisting them into this classic shape.

sugared chocolate pretzels

In a large bowl, cream butter and granulated sugar until fluffy. Add 1 egg and vanilla; beat until smooth. In a small bowl, combine flour, cocoa, baking powder, and salt. Add dry ingredients to creamed mixture; stir until a soft dough forms.

Divide dough into 24 balls. Roll each ball into a 12-inch-long rope, shaping to resemble a pretzel. In a small bowl, whisk remaining egg and water; brush on cookies. Sprinkle with sparkling sugar. Place cookies 2 inches apart on parchment paper-lined baking sheets.

Bake at 350° for 10 to 12 minutes or until edges are slightly firm and bottoms are browned. Cool cookies on baking sheets 2 minutes; transfer to wire racks to cool.

YIELD: *2 dozen pretzels*

$1/2$ cup butter or margarine, softened

$1/2$ cup granulated sugar

2 eggs, divided

1 teaspoon vanilla extract

2 cups all-purpose flour

$1/4$ cup cocoa

1 teaspoon baking powder

$1/4$ teaspoon salt

1 teaspoon water

Coarse white sparkling sugar

HOLIDAYS

Colorful, fun cookies are such an easy way to capture the spirit
of the holidays! Making and sharing Christmas cookies is a huge tradition,
but these homemade sweets are welcome all through the year.
Use them to spread love on Valentine's Day, spark a conversation
on the Fourth of July, treat Halloween goblins, and so much more!

Almost too pretty to eat, Tasty Christmas Wreaths are crafted from twisted ropes
of dough and embellished with a garland of icing and candy holly sprinkles.

tasty christmas wreaths

For cookies, cream butter and sugars in a large bowl until fluffy.
Add egg, lemon zest, and vanilla; beat until smooth. In a small bowl,
combine flour, cornstarch, cardamom, and baking powder. Add dry
ingredients to creamed mixture; stir until a soft dough forms. Place
dough on plastic wrap and shape into four 6-inch-long rolls. Chill
2 hours.

Cut each roll into 12 equal pieces. On a lightly floured surface, roll
each piece into a 6-inch-long rope. Twist 2 ropes of dough together.
Place on greased baking sheets. Shape into wreaths and press ends
together to seal. Bake at 400° for 6 to 8 minutes or until bottoms are
lightly browned. Transfer cookies to wire racks to cool.

For icing, combine confectioners sugar and milk; stir until smooth.
Spoon icing into a pastry bag fitted with a small round tip. Pipe icing
onto wreaths; place holly sprinkles on icing. Allow icing to harden.

YIELD: 2 dozen cookies

COOKIES

- 1/3 **cup butter or margarine, softened**
- 1/3 **cup firmly packed brown sugar**
- 1/2 **cup confectioners sugar**
- 1 **egg**
- 2 **tablespoons grated lemon zest**
- 1/2 **teaspoon vanilla extract**
- 1 1/4 **cups all-purpose flour**
- 1/4 **cup cornstarch**
- 1/2 **teaspoon ground cardamom**
- 1/4 **teaspoon baking powder**

ICING

- 1 **cup confectioners sugar**
- 2 **tablespoons milk**
- **Holly mix sprinkles**

The young—and the young at heart—will enjoy these fun cookies!
The candy canes have a hint of peppermint flavoring, and the reindeer
cookies feature the Christmasy taste of gingerbread.

gingerbread reindeer cookies

In a large bowl, combine gingerbread mix, eggs, oil, and flour; stir until a soft dough forms. For each cookie, place a 1¹/₂-inch ball of dough on a greased baking sheet. Flatten balls into a 3-inch oval shape. Use fingers to press in sides of each cookie about one-third from 1 end of cookie to resemble reindeer face. Press pretzels into cookies for antlers. Press jelly beans into cookies for eyes and noses. Bake at 350° for 9 to 11 minutes or until bottoms of cookies are firm. Transfer cookies to a wire rack to cool.

YIELD: about 1 dozen cookies

1 package (14 ounces) gingerbread mix

2 eggs

2 tablespoons vegetable oil

2 tablespoons all-purpose flour

Small pretzel twists

Black and red jelly beans

peppermint candy cane cookies

In a large bowl, cream butter and sugar until fluffy. Add egg and peppermint extract; beat until smooth. In a medium bowl, combine 2 cups flour, baking powder, and salt. Alternately add dry ingredients and milk to creamed mixture; beat until a soft dough forms. Add remaining ¹/₂ cup flour, using hands to knead until well blended. Divide dough in half; tint half red. Cover with plastic wrap to prevent drying.

For each cookie, shape about 1 teaspoon red dough into a 5-inch-long rope. Repeat with about 1 teaspoon plain dough. Place ropes on ungreased baking sheets. Holding 2 pieces of dough together at ends, twist dough tightly together and press ends together to seal. Shape each cookie to resemble a candy cane, leaving about a 1-inch space in curved part of cookie. Place cookies 1 inch apart. Bake at 350° for 8 to 10 minutes or until lightly browned on bottoms. Cool cookies on baking sheets 1 minute; transfer to wire racks to cool.

YIELD: about 4 dozen cookies

¹/₂ cup butter or margarine, softened

1¹/₄ cups sugar

1 egg

¹/₂ teaspoon peppermint extract

2¹/₂ cups all-purpose flour, divided

1 teaspoon baking powder

¹/₄ teaspoon salt

¹/₄ cup milk

¹/₂ teaspoon red liquid food coloring

If it's just not Christmas without fruitcake, consider these moist cookies instead. The chewy morsels are flavored with semisweet chocolate and chock-full of candied cherries and chopped pecans.

chocolate fruitcake cookies

For cookies, cream butter and sugar in a large bowl until fluffy. Add eggs and vanilla; beat until smooth. Stir in melted chocolate. In a medium bowl, combine flour and baking powder. Add dry ingredients to creamed mixture; stir until a soft dough forms. Stir in cherries and pecans. Drop tablespoonfuls of dough 2 inches apart onto lightly greased baking sheets. Bake at 375° for 6 to 8 minutes or until bottoms are lightly browned. Transfer cookies to wire racks to cool.

For glaze, place chocolate chips and shortening in a small microwave-safe bowl. Microwave on medium-high power (80%) 1 minute; stir. Continue to microwave 15 seconds at a time, stirring until melted. Drizzle glaze over half of cookies; decorate remaining cookies with candied cherry pieces secured with a dot of chocolate glaze.

YIELD: about 4^1/$_2$ dozen cookies

COOKIES

- ^{3}/$_4$ cup butter or margarine, softened
- ^{3}/$_4$ cup sugar
- 2 eggs
- 1 teaspoon vanilla extract
- 2 ounces semisweet baking chocolate, melted
- 2^1/$_4$ cups all-purpose flour
- 1 teaspoon baking powder
- 1 cup coarsely chopped candied red and green cherries
- 1 cup coarsely chopped pecans, toasted

GLAZE

- ^{1}/$_2$ cup semisweet chocolate chips
- 1 teaspoon vegetable shortening

  Green and red candied cherries

Raspberry jam filling enhances the festive look of these Almond Christmas Trees, especially where it peeks out through the "ornament" holes. A dusting of confectioners sugar adds a snowy look.

almond christmas trees

Beat butter, sugar, and egg until light and fluffy. Stir in flour, almonds, extracts, cinnamon, and nutmeg. Divide dough in half and wrap in plastic wrap; chill 30 minutes.

On a lightly floured surface, roll out one half of dough to $1/4$-inch thickness. Using a $4^1/_2$-inch tree-shaped cookie cutter, cut out 24 trees. Place cookies on lightly greased baking sheets.

Roll out remaining half of dough and cut out 24 additional trees. Using a drinking straw, randomly cut a few holes for "ornaments" in second set of cookies. Place cookies on lightly greased baking sheets. If there is any extra dough, roll out and cut an even number of trees, making holes in half of them.

Bake at 375° for 7 to 9 minutes or until lightly browned. Remove from baking sheets and cool on wire racks.

Spread each solid tree with a layer of raspberry jam. Place trees with holes on top of jam layer and dust with confectioners sugar.

YIELD: about 2 dozen cookies

$1^1/_4$ cups butter or margarine, softened

$2/_3$ cup granulated sugar

1 egg

3 cups all-purpose flour

$1^1/_2$ cups finely ground almonds

1 teaspoon vanilla extract

$1/2$ teaspoon almond extract

1 teaspoon ground cinnamon

$1/4$ teaspoon ground nutmeg

Raspberry jam

Confectioners sugar

Alphabet cookie cutters and colorful icing transform these cookies into a fun way to decorate your table with a holiday message. The recipe makes enough for five "Merry Christmas" sets—so you can share or spell out names and other greetings.

"merry christmas" cookies

For cookies, cream butter and confectioners sugar in a large bowl until fluffy. Add egg and almond extract; beat until smooth. In a medium bowl, combine flour and salt. Add dry ingredients to creamed mixture; stir until a soft dough forms. Divide dough in half. Wrap in plastic wrap and chill 1 hour.

On a lightly floured surface, roll out half of dough to $1/4$-inch thickness. Use 2-inch-high alphabet cookie cutters to cut out "Merry Christmas" cookies. Transfer to greased baking sheets. Bake at 350° for 6 to 8 minutes or until edges begin to brown. Transfer cookies to wire racks with waxed paper underneath to cool. Repeat with remaining dough.

For icing, combine water and corn syrup in a heavy medium saucepan. Add confectioners sugar and stir until well blended. Using a pastry brush dipped in hot water, wash down any sugar crystals on sides of pan. Attach a candy thermometer to pan, making sure thermometer does not touch bottom of pan. Stirring constantly and taking care not to scrape sides of pan, cook over medium-low heat until icing reaches 100°. Remove from heat; stir in almond extract and 2 teaspoons half and half. Cool icing 5 minutes. Divide icing evenly into 3 small bowls; tint 1 green and 1 red. If needed, add additional half and half, $1/4$ teaspoon at a time, for desired consistency. Spoon icings over letters. Allow icing to harden.

To decorate, transfer purchased green decorating icing into a decorating bag fitted with a small leaf tip. Transfer red icing into a decorating bag fitted with a very small round tip. Pipe holly leaves, berries, and candy cane stripes onto desired letters. Allow icing to harden. Store in a single layer.

YIELD: about 5 sets of cookies

COOKIES

- $3/4$ cup butter or margarine, softened
- 1 cup confectioners sugar
- 1 egg
- $1 1/2$ teaspoons almond extract
- $2 1/2$ cups all-purpose flour
- $1/4$ teaspoon salt

ICING

- $1/4$ cup water
- 2 tablespoons light corn syrup
- 4 cups confectioners sugar
- $1 1/4$ teaspoons almond extract
- 2 to 3 teaspoons half and half
- Green and red paste food coloring
- Purchased green and red decorating icing

Yielding 19 dozen thin and crispy treats, this recipe is great to use when you plan on packing up lots of little gifts from your kitchen. The cookies keep well in tins and are also good to have on hand for entertaining unexpected guests.

moravian spice cookies

It's best if dough is made in advance.

In a large bowl, cream butter and brown sugar until fluffy. Add molasses; beat until smooth. In a medium bowl, combine flour and remaining ingredients. Gradually add dry ingredients to creamed mixture; stir until a soft dough forms. Divide dough into fourths. Wrap in plastic wrap and chill 48 hours or up to 1 week.

Roll out one fourth of dough at a time to $^1/_{16}$-inch thickness between parchment paper and plastic wrap. Use a 1$^7/_8$-inch-diameter fluted-edge cookie cutter to cut out cookies; remove excess dough. Place parchment paper with cutout cookies on baking sheets. Bake at 350° for 4 to 6 minutes or until edges are lightly browned. Transfer cookies to wire racks to cool.

YIELD: about 19 dozen cookies

$^1/_2$ cup butter or margarine, softened

$^1/_3$ cup firmly packed brown sugar

1 cup molasses

3$^1/_2$ cups all-purpose flour

$^3/_4$ teaspoon baking soda

$^3/_4$ teaspoon ground ginger

$^3/_4$ teaspoon ground cloves

$^3/_4$ teaspoon ground cinnamon

$^1/_4$ teaspoon ground nutmeg

$^1/_4$ teaspoon ground allspice

$^1/_4$ teaspoon salt

Coconut is the common ingredient for these two uncommonly good cookies. It's baked inside the fruity macaroons but takes the spotlight on the candy-coated sandwich cookie "snowballs."

christmas macaroons

In a small bowl, combine $1/4$ cup sugar, flour, and salt. Stir in coconut; set aside.

In a medium bowl, beat egg whites until soft peaks form. Add vanilla. Gradually add remaining 1 cup sugar, beating until mixture is very stiff. Gently fold coconut mixture and candied cherries into egg white mixture.

Drop teaspoonfuls of mixture onto parchment paper-lined baking sheets. Bake at 325° for 15 to 17 minutes or until edges are lightly browned. Transfer cookies to wire racks to cool.

YIELD: about 5 dozen cookies

$1^{1}/_{4}$ cups sugar, divided

$^{1}/_{2}$ cup all-purpose flour

$^{1}/_{4}$ teaspoon salt

$2^{1}/_{2}$ cups sweetened shredded coconut

4 egg whites

$^{1}/_{2}$ teaspoon vanilla extract

1 cup finely chopped green and red candied cherries

snowball cookies

Place coconut in a bowl. Melt candy coating in a heavy medium saucepan over low heat. Remove from heat. Place each cookie on a fork and dip into candy coating until covered; roll in coconut. Place cookies on waxed paper and allow candy coating to harden.

YIELD: about $3^{1}/_{2}$ dozen cookies

3 cups sweetened finely shredded coconut

1 package (18 ounces) vanilla candy coating

1 package (16 ounces) chocolate sandwich cookies

Just as in nature, every one of these "snowflakes" is unique. Dots of piped icing create the frosty patterns.

cinnamon-brown sugar snowflakes

In a large bowl, cream butter and brown sugar until fluffy. Add egg and vanilla; beat until smooth. In a small bowl, combine flour, 1 teaspoon cinnamon, and baking powder. Stir dry ingredients into creamed mixture. Place 1-inch balls of dough 2 inches apart on ungreased baking sheets.

In a small bowl, combine granulated sugar and remaining $1/2$ teaspoon cinnamon. Flatten cookies with a glass dipped in sugar mixture. Bake at 375° for 4 to 6 minutes or until edges are very lightly browned. Transfer cookies to wire racks to cool.

Use icing to pipe desired snowflake designs onto cookies. Allow icing to harden.

YIELD: about $6^{1}/_{2}$ dozen cookies

$3/4$ cup butter or margarine, softened

$1^{1}/_{4}$ cups firmly packed brown sugar

1 egg

1 teaspoon vanilla extract

$1^{3}/_{4}$ cups all-purpose flour

$1^{1}/_{2}$ teaspoons ground cinnamon, divided

1 teaspoon baking powder

2 tablespoons granulated sugar

Purchased white decorating icing

Ring in the New Year with a glass of "bubbly"! For added spirit, flavor the dough with white wine.

new year's toast cookies

For cookies, cream butter and sugar in a large bowl until fluffy. Add wine and egg yolks; beat until smooth. In a small bowl, beat egg whites until soft peaks form. Fold egg whites into creamed mixture. Add flour to creamed mixture, gently stirring until a soft dough forms. Divide dough into half. Wrap in plastic wrap and chill 2 hours.

On a lightly floured surface, roll out one half of dough at a time to $^1/_8$-inch thickness. Use a $1^5/_8$-inch wide x $4^1/_4$-inch-high champagne glass-shaped cookie cutter or pattern on page 141 to cut out cookies. Transfer to lightly greased baking sheets. Bake at 375° for 5 to 7 minutes or until bottoms are lightly browned. Transfer cookies to wire racks to cool.

For icing, combine confectioners sugar, 5 tablespoons milk, and vanilla in a medium bowl; stir until smooth. Add additional milk, $^1/_2$ teaspoon at a time, for desired consistency. Spoon icing into a decorating bag fitted with a small round tip. Pipe icing onto cookies; sprinkle with non-pareils. Allow icing to harden. Store in a single layer.

YIELD: about $6^1/_2$ dozen cookies

COOKIES

- $^3/_4$ cup butter or margarine, softened
- 1 cup sugar
- $^1/_4$ cup white wine or milk
- 2 egg yolks
- 1 egg white
- 3 cups all-purpose flour

ICING

- 4 cups confectioners sugar
- 5 to 6 tablespoons milk
- $^1/_2$ teaspoon vanilla extract
  White non-pareils

For serving up romance on Valentine's Day or any time you want to share a little love, offer these heart-shaped confections. The piped meringues feature cherry flavoring, and the sandwich cookies are filled with raspberry jelly.

sweetheart meringues

Use heart pattern, page 141, and a piece of white paper to trace as many hearts as size of paper will allow, leaving $1/2$ inch between each heart.

In a large bowl, beat egg whites and cream of tartar until soft peaks form. Add cherry flavoring. Gradually add confectioners sugar, beating until mixture is very stiff. Tint pink. Spoon meringue into a large decorating bag fitted with a large open star tip. Place heart patterns under greased waxed paper and pipe meringue onto waxed paper, carefully moving patterns as necessary. Allow cookies to sit at room temperature 30 minutes.

Carefully place waxed paper with hearts on greased baking sheets. Bake at 200° for 2 hours. Leaving cookies on waxed paper, remove waxed paper from baking sheets while cookies are warm; cool. Carefully peel away waxed paper. Store immediately in an airtight container.

YIELD: about $5 1/2$ dozen cookies

- 4 egg whites
- $1/2$ teaspoon cream of tartar
- 1 teaspoon cherry flavoring or extract
- $1 1/2$ cups sifted confectioners sugar
-   Pink paste food coloring

heart cookies

In a medium bowl, cream butter and sugar until fluffy. Add egg and extracts; beat until smooth. In a small bowl, combine flour, cornstarch, baking powder, and salt. Add dry ingredients to creamed mixture; stir until a soft dough forms. On a lightly floured surface, roll out dough to $1/8$-inch thickness. Use a $2 1/4$-inch-wide heart-shaped cookie cutter to cut out cookies. Transfer to greased baking sheets. Use a $3/4$-inch-wide heart-shaped cookie cutter to cut out centers of half of cookies on baking sheets. Bake at 350° for 6 to 9 minutes or until edges are lightly browned. Transfer cookies to wire racks to cool.

Spread a thin layer of raspberry jelly on top of each whole cookie and place a heart cutout cookie on top.

YIELD: about $2 1/2$ dozen cookies

- $3/4$ cup butter or margarine, softened
- $1/2$ cup sugar
- 1 egg
- 1 teaspoon almond extract
- $1/2$ teaspoon vanilla extract
- $1 3/4$ cups all-purpose flour
- 3 tablespoons cornstarch
- $1/2$ teaspoon baking powder
- $1/8$ teaspoon salt
- $1/3$ cup raspberry jelly

If you are really lucky on St. Patrick's Day, you'll discover a pot of Blarney Stones at the end of the rainbow. Loaded with peanuts and golden raisins, the soft, spicy nuggets are worth their weight in gold!

blarney stones

In a large bowl, cream butter and sugar until fluffy. Add eggs and vanilla; beat until smooth. In a small bowl, combine flour, allspice, and baking soda. Add dry ingredients to creamed mixture; stir until a soft dough forms. Stir in peanuts and raisins.

Drop tablespoonfuls of dough 2 inches apart onto greased baking sheets. Bake at 375° for 9 to 12 minutes or until edges are lightly browned. Transfer cookies to wire racks to cool.

YIELD: about 4$\frac{1}{2}$ dozen cookies

$\frac{3}{4}$ cup butter or margarine, softened

1 cup sugar

2 eggs

1$\frac{1}{2}$ teaspoons vanilla extract

1$\frac{3}{4}$ cups all-purpose flour

1 teaspoon ground allspice

$\frac{1}{2}$ teaspoon baking soda

1 can (12 ounces) salted peanuts

1 cup golden raisins

Colorful gourmet jelly beans make perfect "Easter eggs" for these chocolaty coconut "nests." Chopped pecans and graham cracker crumbs help "build" the no-bake treats!

easter egg nests

Combine sweetened condensed milk and chocolate chips in a heavy small saucepan over medium heat. Stirring frequently, heat until chocolate chips are melted. Reduce heat to low. Add coconut, pecans, and cracker crumbs; stir until well blended. Remove from heat.

Drop teaspoonfuls of cookie mixture 1 inch apart onto greased baking sheets. Press 3 jelly beans into center of each cookie. Chill on baking sheets to allow chocolate to harden.

YIELD: about 3$^{1}/_{2}$ dozen cookies

$^{1}/_{2}$ cup plus 2 tablespoons sweetened condensed milk ($^{1}/_{2}$ of a 14-ounce can)

$^{1}/_{4}$ cup semisweet chocolate chips

2 cups sweetened finely shredded coconut

$^{1}/_{2}$ cup finely chopped pecans

$^{1}/_{2}$ cup graham cracker crumbs

4 ounces gourmet jelly beans

The Easter bunny (and other spring visitors) will hop right up for these cake-like Carrot Cookies. Decorated with a sweet glaze and buttercream icing, the spicy cookies are filled with golden raisins, chopped pecans, and fresh carrots.

carrot cookies

For cookies, cream butter and sugar in a large bowl until fluffy. Add eggs and vanilla; beat until smooth. Tint orange. Place carrots, pecans, and raisins in a food processor; process until finely chopped. In a small bowl, combine flour, cornstarch, baking powder, cinnamon, allspice, and salt. Add carrot mixture and dry ingredients to creamed mixture; stir until a soft dough forms. Divide dough into fourths. Wrap in plastic wrap and chill 3 hours or until firm.

On a heavily floured surface, roll out one fourth of dough at a time to $1/4$-inch thickness. Use pattern, page 142, or a $1^3/4$ x $4^3/4$ -inch cookie cutter to cut out cookies. Transfer to ungreased baking sheets. Bake at 375 degrees for 7 to 9 minutes or until edges are lightly browned. Transfer cookies to wire racks with waxed paper underneath to cool.

For glaze, combine confectioners sugar and milk in a small bowl; beat until smooth. Tint orange. Spoon glaze onto large ends of carrot cookies. Allow glaze to harden.

For buttercream icing, combine confectioners sugar, shortening, butter, milk, and vanilla in a small bowl; beat until smooth. Tint green. Spoon icing into a decorating bag fitted with a grass tip. Pipe icing onto tops of cookies to resemble leaves. Allow icing to harden. Store in single layers.

YIELD: about $3^1/2$ dozen cookies

COOKIES

- 1 cup butter, softened
- 1 cup sugar
- 2 eggs
- 2 teaspoons vanilla extract
  Orange paste food coloring
- 3 medium carrots, peeled and quartered
- $1/2$ cup chopped pecans
- $1/2$ cup golden raisins
- $1^3/4$ cups all-purpose flour
- $1/4$ cup cornstarch
- 1 teaspoon baking powder
- 1 teaspoon ground cinnamon
- $3/4$ teaspoon ground allspice
- $1/4$ teaspoon salt

GLAZE

- $1^1/2$ cups confectioners sugar
- 2 tablespoons plus 1 teaspoon milk
  Orange paste food coloring

BUTTERCREAM ICING

- $1^1/2$ cups confectioners sugar
- 3 tablespoons vegetable shortening
- 3 tablespoons butter, softened
- $1^1/2$ tablespoons milk
- $1/2$ teaspoon vanilla extract
  Green paste food coloring

On Mother's Day, these beautifully decorated cookies are a lovely way to remind Mom that she's still the prettiest flower in the garden.

flower baskets

For cookies, beat butter, sugar, sour cream, egg, and almond extract in a large bowl until smooth. In a medium bowl, combine remaining ingredients; add to creamed mixture. Stir until a soft dough forms. Divide dough into thirds. Wrap in plastic wrap and chill overnight.

On a lightly floured surface, roll out one third of dough at a time to $1/4$-inch thickness. Use pattern, page 142, to cut out cookies. Place 2 inches apart on greased baking sheets. Bake at 350° for 8 to 10 minutes or until bottoms are lightly browned. Transfer cookies to wire racks to cool.

For icing, combine first 4 ingredients and 3 tablespoons milk in a large bowl; beat until smooth. To thin icing, add remaining milk 1 teaspoon at a time. In small bowls, tint the icing as follows: $1/4$ cup yellow, $2/3$ cup blue, $2/3$ cup violet, $1/3$ cup green, and remaining icing ivory. Spoon ivory icing into a decorating bag fitted with a basket weave tip (#47). With serrated side of tip up, pipe basket handle onto 1 cookie (***Fig. 1 on page 142***).

Beginning on left side of cookie, pipe a vertical stripe of frosting from middle to bottom edge of cookie. Pipe three $3/4$-inch-long horizontal stripes over vertical stripe about 1 tip width apart. Overlapping ends of horizontal stripes, pipe another vertical stripe to the right of the first vertical stripe (***Fig. 2a on page 142***). Pipe three $3/4$-inch-long horizontal stripes about 1 tip width apart as shown in Fig. 2b on page 142. Repeat basket weave design until lower half of cookie is covered.

Use a medium drop flower tip (#131) and blue icing, and a small drop flower tip (#224) and violet icing to pipe flowers onto cookies. Use a round tip and yellow icing to pipe centers in flowers. Use a small leaf tip (#349) and green icing to pipe leaves onto flowers. Allow icing to harden. Repeat for remaining cookies. Store in a single layer.

YIELD: about 4 dozen cookies

COOKIES

- $1/2$ cup butter, softened
- $3/4$ cup plus 2 tablespoons sugar
- $1/2$ cup sour cream
- 1   egg
- 1   teaspoon almond extract
- $2 1/4$ cups all-purpose flour
- $1/2$ cup slivered almonds, toasted and finely ground
- 1   teaspoon baking powder
- $1/2$ teaspoon baking soda
- $1/4$ teaspoon salt

ICING

- 6   cups confectioners sugar
- $3/4$ cup vegetable shortening
- $3/4$ cup butter, softened
- $1 1/2$ teaspoons almond extract
- 3   to 4 tablespoons milk

   Yellow, blue, violet, green, and ivory paste food coloring

On Father's Day, give Dad a whole batch of these tasty little "neckties." He's sure to love trying them on for size!

nutty neckties

In a large bowl, cream butter, shortening, and brown sugar until fluffy. Add egg and vanilla-butter-nut flavoring; beat until smooth. In a medium bowl, combine flour, baking soda, and salt. Add dry ingredients to creamed mixture; stir until a soft dough forms. Stir in pecans. Divide dough in half. Wrap in plastic wrap and chill 2 hours.

On a lightly floured surface, roll out one half of dough at a time to $1/4$-inch thickness. Use pattern, page 142, to cut out cookies. Use food coloring and a small paintbrush to paint red and blue diagonal stripes on cookies. Place 2 inches apart on ungreased baking sheets. Bake at 375° for 7 to 9 minutes or until bottoms are lightly browned. Transfer to wire racks to cool.

YIELD: $1^1/2$ dozen cookies

$1/2$ cup butter or margarine, softened

$1/4$ cup vegetable shortening

$1^1/4$ cups firmly packed brown sugar

1 egg

1 teaspoon vanilla-butter-nut flavoring

$2^1/4$ cups all-purpose flour

$1/2$ teaspoon baking soda

$1/4$ teaspoon salt

$3/4$ cup chopped pecans, toasted and finely ground

Red and blue liquid food coloring

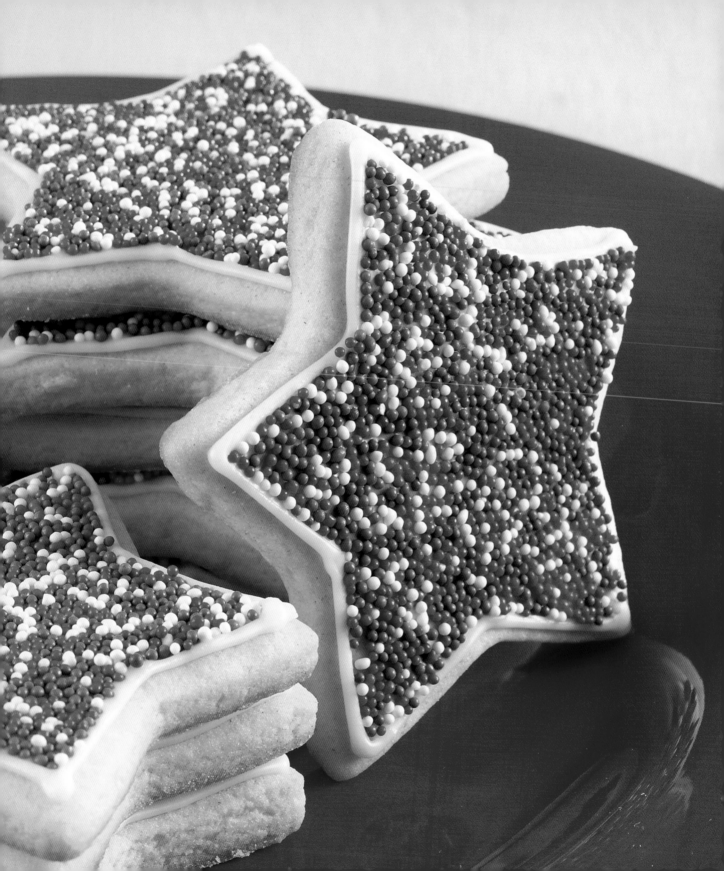

For the Fourth of July, red, white, and blue non-pareils make it easy to give patriotic pizzazz to these buttery cookies. A piped icing outline helps define the star shapes.

star-spangled cookies

For cookies, cream butter and sugars in a large bowl until fluffy. Add egg, vanilla, and butter flavoring; beat until smooth. In a medium bowl, combine flour, cornstarch, and salt. Add dry ingredients to creamed mixture; stir until a soft dough forms. Divide dough in half. Wrap in plastic wrap and chill 2 hours.

On a lightly floured surface, roll out half of dough at a time to $^1/_4$-inch thickness. Use a 3-inch star-shaped cookie cutter to cut out cookies. Place 2 inches apart on greased baking sheets. Bake at 350° for 8 to 10 minutes or until bottoms are lightly browned. Transfer cookies to wire racks to cool.

For icing, combine confectioners sugar, 2 tablespoons plus 2 teaspoons milk, and vanilla in a small bowl; stir until smooth. Place $^1/_2$ cup icing in another small bowl and add remaining 2 teaspoons milk to thin; cover and set aside.

Spoon remaining icing into a decorating bag fitted with a small round tip. Pipe outline onto each cookie. Allow icing to harden. Using a small paintbrush, paint reserved thinned icing inside piped lines on tops of cookies. Sprinkle non-pareils over cookies before icing hardens. Allow icing to harden.

YIELD: about 3$^1/_2$ dozen cookies

COOKIES

- $^3/_4$ cup butter or margarine, softened
- $^1/_2$ cup granulated sugar
- $^1/_2$ cup sifted confectioners sugar
- 1 egg
- 2 teaspoons vanilla extract
- 1 teaspoon liquid butter flavoring
- 2$^1/_4$ cups all-purpose flour
- 2 tablespoons cornstarch
- $^1/_4$ teaspoon salt

ICING

- 2 cups confectioners sugar
- 3 tablespoons plus 1 teaspoon milk, divided
- $^1/_2$ teaspoon clear vanilla extract (used in cake decorating)

  Red, white, and blue non-pareils

These colorful cookies will be a sweet surprise at all kinds of summer celebrations. Watermelon-flavored gelatin provides authentic taste, while chocolate chip "seeds" and green sugar "rinds" complete the look.

watermelon slices

In a large bowl, cream butter, granulated sugar, and gelatin until fluffy. Add egg and vanilla; beat until smooth. Tint pink. In a medium bowl, combine flour, cornstarch, and baking powder. Add dry ingredients to creamed mixture; stir until a soft dough forms. Stir in chocolate chips. Shape dough into four 8-inch-long rolls. Wrap in plastic wrap and chill 2 hours.

In a small bowl, combine decorating sugars. Coat each roll in decorating sugar. Cut dough into $1/2$-inch-thick slices. Place 2 inches apart on greased baking sheets. Bake at 350° for 10 to 12 minutes or until bottoms are lightly browned. Transfer cookies to wire racks to cool.

YIELD: about $6^1/2$ dozen cookies

$1^1/2$ cups butter or margarine, softened

1 cup granulated sugar

2 packages (3 ounces each) watermelon-flavored gelatin

1 egg

1 teaspoon vanilla extract

Pink paste food coloring

$3^1/4$ cups all-purpose flour

$1/4$ cup cornstarch

1 teaspoon baking powder

1 cup semisweet chocolate mini chips

5 tablespoons green decorating sugar

5 teaspoons yellow decorating sugar

These spooky cookies are sure to be a "scream" at Halloween parties!
Gummy spiders provide the finishing touch for the web-inspired treats.

spiderweb cookies

For cookies, cream butter and sugar in a large bowl until fluffy. Add eggs
and vanilla; beat until smooth. In a medium bowl, combine flour and
cocoa. Add dry ingredients to creamed mixture; beat until well blended.
Shape dough into thirty 1$^1/_2$-inch-diameter balls and place 2 inches apart
on lightly greased baking sheets; flatten balls into 3-inch circles with
bottom of a lightly greased glass. Bake at 350 for 9 to 11 minutes or until
bottoms are lightly browned. Cool cookies on baking sheets 2 minutes;
transfer to wire racks to cool.

For icing, place confectioners sugar in a medium bowl; add vanilla and
gradually stir in milk until icing is desired spreading consistency. Cover
and set aside. Place chocolate chips in a small microwave-safe bowl.
Microwave on high power (100%) 1 minute or until chocolate softens;
stir until smooth. Spoon melted chocolate into a decorating bag fitted
with a small round tip. Working with 2 cookies at a time, spread icing
on cookies. Beginning at center of each cookie, pipe 3 or 4 chocolate
circles, one outside the other and about $^1/_4$-inch apart, onto wet icing.
Beginning at smallest circle, pull a toothpick through circles to outer
edge of icing to make spiderweb design. Decorate cookies with candy
spiders. Repeat with remaining cookies, icing, and chocolate. Allow icing
to harden.

YIELD: 30 cookies

COOKIES

- 1$^1/_3$ cups butter or margarine, softened
- 1$^1/_3$ cups sugar
- 2 eggs
- 1$^1/_2$ teaspoons vanilla extract
- 3$^1/_3$ cups all-purpose flour
- $^1/_3$ cup cocoa

ICING AND SPIDERWEBS

- 4$^1/_2$ cups confectioners sugar
- 1$^1/_2$ teaspoons vanilla extract
- $^1/_3$ cup plus 1 teaspoon milk
- $^1/_2$ cup semisweet chocolate chips
- Gummy spiders

Conjure up some Halloween treats with a batch of Orange Slice Cookies. Big chunks of chewy gumdrop candies make them extra delicious.

orange slice cookies

In a large bowl, cream butter and sugars until fluffy. Add egg and vanilla; beat until smooth. In a small bowl, combine flour, baking powder, and salt. Add dry ingredients to creamed mixture; stir until a soft dough forms. Stir in candy pieces. Shape dough into three 9-inch-long rolls. Wrap in plastic wrap and chill 3 hours or until firm enough to handle.

Cut dough into $1/4$-inch-thick slices. Place 1 inch apart on lightly greased baking sheets. Bake at 375° for 6 to 8 minutes or until edges are lightly browned. Transfer cookies to wire racks to cool.

YIELD: about 6 dozen cookies

$3/4$ cup butter or margarine, softened

1 cup granulated sugar

$1/2$ cup firmly packed brown sugar

1 egg

1 teaspoon vanilla extract

$1^3/4$ cups all-purpose flour

$1/2$ teaspoon baking powder

$1/2$ teaspoon salt

2 cups orange slice gumdrop candies, quartered

Bake up a basketful of leaf-shaped cookies in honor of the glorious fall foliage! You'll feel like Jack Frost as you paint the maple-flavored cutouts with vivid food coloring.

maple leaves

In a large bowl, cream butter, shortening, and sugar until fluffy. Add syrup, eggs, maple flavoring, and vanilla; beat until smooth. In another large bowl, combine flour and salt. Add dry ingredients to creamed mixture; stir until a soft dough forms.

On a lightly floured surface, roll out dough to $1/4$-inch thickness. Use a $3 \times 2^1/_2$-inch maple leaf-shaped cookie cutter to cut out cookies. Transfer to greased baking sheets. Bake at 350° for 7 to 9 minutes or until bottoms are lightly browned. Transfer cookies to wire racks to cool.

Place 1 tablespoon water in each of 6 small bowls. Tint each bowl of water with a small amount of food coloring. To decorate cookies, use a small paintbrush to lightly brush diluted food coloring onto cookies to resemble fall leaves. Allow to dry.

YIELD: about 9 dozen cookies

1 cup butter or margarine, softened

$2/_3$ cup vegetable shortening

2 cups sugar

$1/_2$ cup maple syrup

2 eggs

1 teaspoon maple flavoring

1 teaspoon vanilla extract

6 cups all-purpose flour

$1/_2$ teaspoon salt

6 tablespoons water

Orange, green, yellow, copper, brown, and red paste food coloring

Pumpkin Spice Bars are an easy dessert for Thanksgiving. Made using
a cake mix and canned pumpkin, the creamy bars feature a spice-cake crust.

pumpkin spice bars

In a large bowl, combine cake mix, 1 egg, and melted butter; stir until
mixture is well blended (mixture will be dry). Press into bottoms of three
8 x 5 x 1-inch aluminum foil pans or one $10^1/_2$ x $15^1/_2$ x 1-inch jellyroll pan.

In another large bowl, beat cream cheese until fluffy. Add sweetened
condensed milk, pumpkin, 2 eggs, and salt; beat until mixture is smooth.
Pour over crust. Sprinkle pecans over filling. Bake at 350° for 30 to
35 minutes or until filling is set. Cool in pan on a wire rack 20 minutes;
chill. Cut into $1^1/_2$-inch bars. Store in refrigerator.

YIELD: about 5 dozen bars

1 package (18.25 ounces)
  spice cake mix

1 egg

2 tablespoons butter or
  margarine, melted

1 package (8 ounces)
  cream cheese, softened

1 can (14 ounces)
  sweetened condensed
  milk

1 can (16 ounces) pumpkin

2 eggs

$1/_2$ teaspoon salt

1 cup chopped pecans

ELEGANT CLASSICS

Whether you're hosting a big open house, a small reception,
or a formal dinner, our gourmet confections will delight your guests
with discriminating tastes. This sweet assortment is laced
with intense flavors and scrumptious nuts to please adult palates.

Serve these beautiful brownies every time you want to make a grand impression!
A swirl of raspberry jam glamorizes their rich cream cheese topping.

raspberry-cream cheese brownies

For topping, beat cream cheese and sugar in a medium bowl until smooth. Add egg and vanilla; beat until well blended. Set aside.

For brownies, beat butter and sugar in a large bowl until fluffy. Add eggs, 1 at a time, continuing to beat after each addition. Add melted chocolate, vanilla, and flour; stir until well blended. Spread chocolate mixture into 2 greased 8-inch square baking pans. Spread cream cheese mixture over chocolate mixture. Spoon jam over cream cheese mixture. Use a knife to swirl jam through cream cheese mixture.

Bake at 350° for 38 to 40 minutes or until center is almost set. Cool in pans. Cut into 1¹/₂-inch squares.

YIELD: about 25 brownies in each pan

TOPPING

- 11 ounces cream cheese, softened
- ¹/₃ cup sugar
- 1 egg
- 1 teaspoon vanilla extract

BROWNIES

- 1 cup butter, softened
- 1²/₃ cups sugar
- 3 eggs
- 6 ounces semisweet baking chocolate, melted
- 2 teaspoons vanilla extract
- 1³/₄ cups all-purpose flour
- ¹/₂ cup seedless raspberry jam

Honey-sweetened pistachios and tender, lemony dough all rolled up together—
these are no ordinary slice-and-bake cookies! The colorful treats are sure to
make your list of fancy favorites.

pistachio swirls

In a large bowl, cream butter and sugar until fluffy. Add egg, lemon juice,
lemon zest, and vanilla; beat until smooth. In a small bowl, combine flour
and salt. Add dry ingredients to creamed mixture; stir until a soft dough
forms. Divide dough in half. Wrap in plastic wrap and chill 2 hours or
until firm enough to handle.

In a small bowl, combine pistachio nuts and honey. Roll out half of
dough between sheets of plastic wrap into an 8 x 10-inch rectangle.
Spread dough with half of pistachio mixture to within $1/2$ inch of edges.
Beginning at 1 long edge, roll up dough jellyroll style. Repeat with
remaining dough and pistachio mixture. Wrap rolls in plastic wrap and
chill 2 hours or until firm enough to slice.

If rolls have flattened on the bottom, reshape into a round shape. Using
a serrated knife, cut dough into $1/4$-inch-thick slices. Place 1 inch apart
on ungreased baking sheets. Bake at 375° for 9 to 11 minutes or until
bottoms are lightly browned. Transfer cookies to wire racks to cool.

YIELD: about 5 dozen cookies

$3/4$ cup butter or margarine, softened

$1/2$ cup sugar

1 egg

1 tablespoon lemon juice

$1/2$ teaspoon lemon zest

$1/2$ teaspoon vanilla extract

$1^3/4$ cups all-purpose flour

$1/4$ teaspoon salt

$1^1/4$ cups finely chopped pistachio nuts

$1/4$ cup honey

Finely ground almonds lend mild flavor to these light, chewy cookies. Whole almonds top off their picture-perfect look.

turkish almond cookies

Place slivered almonds in a food processor; process until almost finely ground. Add confectioners sugar; process until well blended. In a heavy medium saucepan, combine sugar mixture and egg whites. Attach a candy thermometer to saucepan, making sure thermometer does not touch bottom of pan. Stirring frequently, cook over medium heat until mixture reaches 130°. Pour into a medium bowl and cool to room temperature.

Spoon mixture into a pastry bag fitted with a medium round tip. Pipe 1-inch-diameter cookies 2 inches apart onto parchment paper-lined baking sheets. Place a whole almond on top of each cookie. Bake at 300° for 20 to 25 minutes or until tops are lightly browned. Cool cookies on baking sheets 5 minutes; transfer to wire racks to cool.

YIELD: about 4 dozen cookies

1 cup slivered almonds
2 cups confectioners sugar
3 egg whites
   Whole almonds

Mouthwatering chocolate meets bold cherry flavor in these irresistible iced brownies. Dried cherries soaked in cherry liqueur enhance the moist treats.

black forest brownies

For brownies, combine cherries and kirsch in a small bowl; allow to stand 30 minutes.

In a large bowl, combine brownie mix, oil, eggs, water, and cherry mixture; stir until well blended. Line a 9 x 13-inch baking pan with aluminum foil, extending foil over ends of pan; grease foil. Spread batter into prepared pan. Bake at 350° for 20 to 25 minutes or until brownies start to pull away from sides of pan. Place pan on a wire rack to cool. Use foil to lift brownies from pan.

For icing, melt chocolate chips and butter in a heavy small saucepan over low heat, stirring frequently. Remove from heat. Add corn syrup and kirsch; beat until smooth. Spread warm icing over brownies; allow icing to harden. Cut into 1^1/$_2$ x 2-inch bars.

YIELD: about 3^1/$_2$ dozen brownies

BROWNIES

- ^{3}/$_4$ cup dried cherries
- 3 tablespoons kirsch (cherry liqueur)
- 1 package (19.8 ounces) brownie mix
- ^{1}/$_3$ cup vegetable oil
- 2 eggs, beaten
- 2 tablespoons water

ICING

- 1 package (6 ounces) semisweet chocolate chips
- 2 tablespoons butter or margarine
- 2 tablespoons light corn syrup
- 2 tablespoons kirsch (cherry liqueur)

Shaped like the familiar childhood toy, these soft cookies enfold a zesty filling of dates simmered in orange juice. The pretty edges of the cinnamon-spiced dough are cut using a pastry wheel.

date-filled pinwheels

For cookies, cream butter and sugars until fluffy. Add eggs and vanilla; beat until smooth. In a medium bowl, combine dry ingredients and add to creamed mixture; stir until a soft dough forms. Divide dough into fourths. Wrap in plastic wrap and chill 2 hours.

For filling, combine all ingredients in a heavy medium saucepan over medium heat. Stirring frequently, cook 8 minutes or until mixture thickens. Set aside.

On a well floured surface, roll out one fourth of dough at a time to $1/8$-inch thickness. Using a pastry wheel, cut dough into $2^1/2$-inch squares; place 1 inch apart on greased baking sheets. Use pastry wheel to make a 1-inch cut from each corner toward the center of each square. Place $1/2$ teaspoon of date mixture in center of square. Bring every other dough corner toward the center of cookie, leaving filling slightly uncovered. Chill cookies 45 minutes.

Bake at 350° for 6 to 8 minutes or until edges are lightly browned. Transfer cookies to wire racks to cool.

YIELD: about 6 dozen cookies

COOKIES

- 1 cup butter or margarine, softened
- 1 cup granulated sugar
- 1 cup firmly packed brown sugar
- 3 eggs
- $1/2$ teaspoon vanilla extract
- $3^1/2$ cups all-purpose flour
- 1 teaspoon baking soda
- 1 teaspoon ground cinnamon
- $1/4$ teaspoon salt

FILLING

- 12 ounces dates, finely chopped
- 6 tablespoons sugar
- 6 tablespoons orange juice
- 2 teaspoons grated orange zest

Kissed with a splash of bourbon and rolled in toasted pecans, tender Chocolate-Nut Truffle Cookies are an irresistible treat. Semisweet baking chocolate and sour cream flavor the contrasting colors of dough in the Buttery Spirals.

chocolate-nut truffle cookies

In a heavy medium saucepan, combine $1/4$ cup butter, whipping cream, and honey over medium-low heat. Stirring frequently, heat mixture to a simmer. Remove from heat. Add chocolate chips; stir until smooth. Stir in bourbon and vanilla. In a large bowl, cream remaining $3/4$ cup butter and confectioners sugar until fluffy. In a medium bowl, combine flour, nutmeg, and salt. Add dry ingredients and chocolate mixture to creamed mixture; stir until a soft dough forms. Cover dough and chill 1 hour.

Shape dough into 1-inch balls and roll in pecans. Transfer to ungreased baking sheets. Bake at 375° for 6 to 8 minutes or until firm. Transfer cookies to wire racks to cool.

YIELD: about $6^1/2$ dozen cookies

- 1 cup butter or margarine, softened and divided
- $1/4$ cup whipping cream
- 2 tablespoons honey
- 1 package (6 ounces) semisweet chocolate chips
- 2 tablespoons bourbon
- 1 teaspoon vanilla extract
- $1/2$ cup confectioners sugar
- $2^1/4$ cups all-purpose flour
- $1/4$ teaspoon ground nutmeg
- $1/4$ teaspoon salt
- $1^1/2$ cups chopped pecans, toasted and coarsely ground

buttery spirals

Place flour in a medium bowl. Using a pastry blender or 2 knives, cut in butter until mixture resembles coarse meal. Stir in sour cream and vanilla. Divide dough in half. Add melted chocolate to half of dough. Divide plain and chocolate doughs in half. Wrap in plastic wrap and chill 2 hours.

Between pieces of plastic wrap sprinkled with sugar, roll out half of plain dough into a 6 x 10-inch rectangle. Repeat to roll out half of chocolate dough. Using plastic wrap, place chocolate dough on top of plain dough. Beginning at 1 long edge, roll up dough jellyroll style. Wrap roll in plastic wrap. Repeat with remaining doughs. Chill 1 hour.

Cut dough into $1/2$-inch-thick slices. Place 2 inches apart on parchment paper-lined baking sheets. Lightly sprinkle cookies with sugar. Bake at 375° for 12 minutes. Turn cookies over, sprinkle with sugar, and bake an additional 2 to 3 minutes. Transfer cookies to wire racks to cool.

YIELD: about 3 dozen cookies

- $1^1/2$ cups all-purpose flour
- 1 cup chilled butter
- $1/2$ cup sour cream
- 1 teaspoon vanilla extract
- 2 ounces semisweet baking chocolate, melted
  Sugar

Traditional Hanukkah pastries, crescent-shaped Rugelach present a pleasing filling of raisins and walnuts rolled in a flaky cream cheese dough. The taste is unforgettable!

rugelach

For dough, beat cream cheese, butter, sugar, and vanilla in a medium bowl until fluffy. Add flour; stir until a soft dough forms. Divide dough into 3 balls. Wrap in plastic wrap and chill overnight.

For filling, combine raisins, sugars, and cinnamon in a food processor; process until raisins are coarsely chopped. Add walnuts and continue to process until walnuts are finely chopped.

On a heavily floured surface, roll out 1 ball of dough into a 12-inch circle. Spread 1 tablespoon butter over dough circle. Sprinkle about 9 tablespoons filling over buttered dough; press lightly into dough. Using a pizza cutter, cut dough into quarters; cut each quarter into 3 wedges. Beginning at wide end, roll up each wedge. Transfer to parchment paper-lined baking sheets.

Bake at 350° for 15 to 20 minutes or until edges are lightly browned. Transfer cookies to wire racks to cool. Repeat with remaining dough and filling.

YIELD: 3 dozen cookies

DOUGH

- 1 package (8 ounces) cream cheese, softened
- 3/4 cup butter or margarine, softened
- 2 tablespoons sugar
- 1 teaspoon vanilla extract
- 1 1/2 cups all-purpose flour

FILLING

- 3/4 cup raisins
- 1/4 cup granulated sugar
- 1/4 cup firmly packed brown sugar
- 1 1/2 teaspoons ground cinnamon
- 1 cup coarsely chopped walnuts, toasted
- 3 tablespoons butter or margarine, softened and divided

Rich raspberry jam and sliced almonds are the crowning touch for these wonderful bars. Cinnamon, allspice, and lemon zest spice up the dense cookies.

austrian linzer bars

In a large bowl, cream butter and sugar until fluffy. Add egg yolks, lemon zest, and vanilla; beat until smooth. In a small bowl, combine flour, cinnamon, baking powder, and allspice. Add dry ingredients to creamed mixture; stir until a soft dough forms. Stir in ground almonds.

Press dough into a greased 9 x 13-inch baking pan. Spread raspberry jam over dough. Sprinkle coarsely chopped almonds over jam.

Bake at 375° for 28 to 30 minutes or until edges are browned. Cool in pan. Cut into 1 x 2-inch bars.

YIELD: about 4 dozen bars

1 cup butter or margarine, softened

$^3/_4$ cup sugar

2 egg yolks

1 tablespoon grated lemon zest

1 teaspoon vanilla extract

2 cups all-purpose flour

1 teaspoon ground cinnamon

$^1/_2$ teaspoon baking powder

$^1/_2$ teaspoon ground allspice

1 cup sliced almonds, finely ground

1 cup seedless raspberry jam

1 cup sliced almonds, coarsely chopped

A French favorite, Chocolate Madeleines are delicious sponge cake morsels laced with cherry liqueur. Tradition calls for baking them in ribbed pans shaped like seashells.

chocolate madeleines

In a large bowl, beat granulated sugar, eggs, and egg yolks 5 minutes or until mixture is thick and light in color. Stir in kirsch and vanilla. In a small bowl, combine flour, cocoa, and salt. Sift dry ingredients over egg mixture; fold in dry ingredients. Fold melted butter into batter.

Spoon 1 tablespoon of batter into each greased 2 x 3-inch mold of a madeleine pan. Bake at 400° for 6 to 8 minutes or until madeleines spring back when lightly touched. Transfer to wire racks. Lightly sift confectioners sugar over warm madeleines; cool.

YIELD: about 2^1/$_2$ dozen madeleines

^{3}/$_4$ cup granulated sugar

2 eggs

2 egg yolks

2 tablespoons kirsch (cherry liqueur)

1 teaspoon vanilla extract

1 cup all-purpose flour

^{1}/$_4$ cup Dutch process cocoa

^{1}/$_8$ teaspoon salt

^{1}/$_2$ cup butter or margarine, melted and cooled

Confectioners sugar

HEALTHY CHOICES

We've always known that cookies are **good**, but with these special recipes, they can also be **good for you**. And you don't have to sacrifice taste! Our food editors found some smart ways to cut calories and fat while still packing the cookies with flavor.

Want a way to take your morning raisin bran on the run? Grab a handful of these yummy cookies! They're packed with your favorite cereal... and they're so much more fun to eat!

raisin-nut chewies

In a medium bowl, beat egg whites until soft peaks form. Gradually add sugar, beating until mixture is very stiff. Fold in cereal and pecans. Drop teaspoonfuls of mixture 1 inch apart onto parchment paper-lined baking sheets. Bake at 200° for 1 hour or until bottoms are lightly browned. Transfer cookies to wire racks to cool.

YIELD: about 3$1/2$ dozen cookies

1 SERVING (1 COOKIE): 26 calories, 0.6 gram fat, 0.5 gram protein, 5.2 grams carbohydrate

- 2 egg whites
- $1/2$ cup sugar
- 2$1/2$ cups raisin bran cereal
- $1/3$ cup chopped pecans, toasted and coarsely ground

These treats are so unbelievably delicious, no one will guess that they are made with health-conscious ingredients. Orange marmalade adds moistness to the brownies and refreshing flavor to the creamy icing.

moist and chewy brownies

For brownies, beat oil and sugars in a large bowl until well blended. Add egg substitute, evaporated milk, corn syrup, marmalade, and vanilla; beat until smooth. In a small bowl, combine flour, cocoa, and salt. Add dry ingredients to sugar mixture; stir until well blended. Line a 9-inch square baking pan with aluminum foil, extending foil over opposite sides of pan; spray foil with cooking spray. Pour batter into prepared pan. Bake at 350° for 34 to 36 minutes or until brownies pull away from sides of pan. Cool in pan. Use foil to lift brownies from pan.

For icing, combine all ingredients in a small bowl. Spread icing over brownies. Cleaning knife frequently, cut into 1^1/$_2$-inch squares. Store in a single layer.

YIELD: about 2^1/$_2$ dozen brownies

1 SERVING (1 BROWNIE): 92 calories, 2 grams fat, 1.0 gram protein, 18 grams carbohydrate

BROWNIES

- ^{1}/$_4$ cup vegetable oil
- 1 cup granulated sugar
- ^{1}/$_2$ cup firmly packed brown sugar
- ^{1}/$_2$ cup egg substitute (equivalent to 2 eggs)
- ^{1}/$_4$ cup evaporated skimmed milk
- 2 tablespoons light corn syrup
- 2 tablespoons orange marmalade
- 1 teaspoon vanilla extract
- 1^1/$_4$ cups all-purpose flour
- ^{1}/$_4$ cup cocoa
- ^{1}/$_4$ teaspoon salt
  Vegetable cooking spray

ICING

- ^{1}/$_2$ cup confectioners sugar
- 2 tablespoons orange marmalade
- 1 tablespoon cocoa
- 1 teaspoon skim milk
- ^{1}/$_2$ teaspoon vanilla extract

An apple a day keeps the doctor away…so they say!…and these great-tasting apple-rich cookies are another way to stay healthy. The naturally good snacks are chock-full of old-fashioned oats, fresh apple, prunes, and toasted pecans.

fruity oatmeal cookies

Combine prunes, apple, and hot water in food processor; process until smooth. In a large bowl, beat sugar, egg substitute, oil, and vanilla until well blended. Add prune mixture. In a small bowl, combine flour, cinnamon, baking soda, baking powder, and salt. Add dry ingredients to sugar mixture; stir until well blended. Stir in oats and pecans.

Drop heaping teaspoonfuls of dough 2 inches apart onto baking sheets lightly sprayed with cooking spray. Bake at 375° for 7 to 9 minutes or until edges are lightly browned. Transfer cookies to wire racks to cool.

YIELD: about 6 dozen cookies

1 SERVING (1 COOKIE): 55 calories, 1.4 grams fat, 1.1 grams protein, 9.7 grams carbohydrate

1/2 cup pitted prunes

1 medium Granny Smith apple, peeled, cored, and diced

1/4 cup hot water

1 1/2 cups sugar

1/2 cup egg substitute (equivalent to 2 eggs)

1/4 cup vegetable oil

1 teaspoon vanilla extract

2 cups all-purpose flour

1 teaspoon ground cinnamon

1 teaspoon baking soda

1/2 teaspoon baking powder

1/2 teaspoon salt

3 cups old-fashioned oats, toasted

1/3 cup chopped pecans, toasted

Vegetable cooking spray

Orange juice is a favorite way to start the day, and after one taste of these zesty squares, you'll want to add them to your daily routine. Drizzled with fruity icing, they are bursting with the sweet, tangy taste of fresh cranberries and oranges.

cranberry-orange squares

Combine cranberries and $1/4$ cup granulated sugar in food processor. Process until cranberries are coarsely chopped. In a small bowl, combine remaining 1 cup granulated sugar, flour, cornstarch, baking soda, and salt. Add buttermilk, 2 tablespoons orange juice, egg whites, and orange zest to dry ingredients; stir until well blended. Stir in cranberry mixture.

Line a 9 x 13-inch baking pan with waxed paper; lightly spray paper with cooking spray. Spread mixture into prepared pan. Bake at 350° for 20 to 25 minutes or until lightly browned. Cool in pan on a wire rack.

Combine confectioners sugar and remaining $2^1/2$ tablespoons orange juice in a small bowl; stir until smooth. Drizzle icing over top. Allow icing to harden. Cut into $1^1/2$-inch squares.

YIELD: about 4 dozen squares

1 SERVING (1 SQUARE): 46 calories, 0.2 gram fat, 0.4 gram protein, 9.8 grams carbohydrate

1	cup fresh cranberries
$1^1/4$	cups granulated sugar, divided
1	cup all-purpose flour
$1/4$	cup cornstarch
$1/2$	teaspoon baking soda
$1/2$	teaspoon salt
$1/2$	cup nonfat buttermilk
$4^1/2$	tablespoons orange juice, divided
2	egg whites
1	teaspoon grated orange zest
	Vegetable cooking spray
1	cup confectioners sugar

So pretty…so light…so good! You won't be able to resist these cookies… and you won't have to, because they are so low in calories and fat. Made with nonfat cream cheese and egg whites, their big flavor comes from lemon zest and spicy cardamom.

lemon-cardamom drops

For cookies, beat cream cheese, butter, and 1 cup sugar in a large bowl until fluffy. Add egg whites, lemon zest, and extracts; beat until smooth. In a medium bowl, combine flour, baking powder, and cardamom. Add dry ingredients to creamed mixture; stir until a soft dough forms.

Place remaining $1/4$ cup sugar in a small bowl. Drop teaspoonfuls of dough into sugar; roll dough into balls. Place balls 2 inches apart on baking sheets lightly sprayed with cooking spray; flatten balls with bottom of a glass dipped in sugar. Bake at 350° for 5 to 7 minutes or until bottoms are lightly browned. Transfer cookies to wire racks with waxed paper underneath to cool.

For icing, combine all ingredients in a small bowl; stir until smooth. Place icing in a small resealable plastic bag. Snip off 1 bottom corner of bag; drizzle over cookies. Allow icing to harden.

YIELD: about 6 dozen cookies

1 SERVING (1 COOKIE): 37 calories, 0.4 gram fat, 0.7 gram protein, 7.6 grams carbohydrate

COOKIES

- 4 ounces ($1/2$ of an 8-ounce package) nonfat cream cheese, softened
- 2 tablespoons butter, softened
- $1^1/4$ cups sugar, divided
- 2 egg whites
- 1 tablespoon grated lemon zest
- 1 teaspoon vanilla extract
- $1/2$ teaspoon lemon extract
- $2^1/4$ cups all-purpose flour
- $3/4$ teaspoon baking powder
- $1/2$ teaspoon ground cardamom
- Vegetable cooking spray

ICING

- $3/4$ cup confectioners sugar
- 3 teaspoons skim milk
- $1/4$ teaspoon vanilla extract

No, you're not dreaming…these chocolate chip cookies truly qualify as a healthy choice. A few smart substitutions make a big difference in the nutrition count, so you don't have to feel guilty about treating yourself!

chocolate-oat bars

In a large bowl, beat oil and sugars until well blended. Add egg whites and vanilla; beat until smooth. In a small bowl, combine flour, oats, baking soda, and salt. Add dry ingredients to sugar mixture; stir until well blended.

Press dough into a 9 x 13-inch baking pan lightly sprayed with cooking spray. Sprinkle chocolate chips over top; lightly press into dough. Bake at 375° for 8 to 10 minutes or until lightly browned. Cool in pan. Cut into 1 x 2-inch bars.

YIELD: about 4 dozen bars

1 SERVING (1 BAR): 59 calories, 2 grams fat, 0.6 gram protein, 7.5 grams carbohydrate

$1/4$ cup vegetable oil

$3/4$ cup firmly packed brown sugar

$1/3$ cup granulated sugar

2 egg whites

2 teaspoons vanilla extract

$1 1/2$ cups all-purpose flour

1 cup quick-cooking oats

$1/2$ teaspoon baking soda

$1/8$ teaspoon salt

Vegetable cooking spray

$1/2$ cup semisweet chocolate mini chips

KITCHEN TIPS

MEASURING INGREDIENTS

Liquid measuring cups have a rim above the measuring line to keep liquid ingredients from spilling. Nested measuring cups are used to measure dry ingredients, butter, shortening, and peanut butter. Measuring spoons are used for measuring both dry and liquid ingredients.

To measure flour or granulated sugar: Spoon ingredient into nested measuring cup and level off with a knife. Do not pack down with spoon.

To measure confectioners sugar: Sift sugar, spoon lightly into nested measuring cup, and level off with a knife.

To measure brown sugar: Pack sugar into nested measuring cup and level off with a knife. Sugar should hold its shape when removed from cup.

To measure butter, shortening, or peanut butter: Pack ingredient firmly into nested measuring cup and level off with a knife.

To measure liquids: Use a liquid measuring cup placed on a flat surface. Pour ingredient into cup and check measuring line at eye level.

To measure honey or syrup: For a more accurate measurement, lightly spray measuring cup or spoon with cooking spray before measuring so the liquid will release easily from cup or spoon.

SOFTENING BUTTER OR MARGARINE

To soften butter, remove wrapper from butter and place on a microwave-safe plate. Microwave 1 stick 20 to 30 seconds at medium-low power (30%).

SOFTENING CREAM CHEESE

To soften cream cheese, remove wrapper from cream cheese and place on a microwave-safe plate. Microwave 1 to 1 1/2 minutes at medium power (50%) for an 8 ounce package or 30 to 45 seconds for a 3-ounce package.

WHIPPING CREAM

For greatest volume, chill a glass bowl, beaters, and cream until well chilled before whipping. In warm weather, place chilled bowl over ice while whipping cream.

TOASTING NUTS

To toast nuts, spread nuts on an ungreased baking sheet. Stirring occasionally, bake 8 to 10 minutes in a preheated 350-degree oven until nuts are slightly darker in color.

PREPARING CITRUS FRUIT ZEST

To remove outer portion of peel (colored part) from citrus fruits, use a fine grater or fruit zester, being careful not to cut into the bitter white portion. Zest is also referred to as grated peel.

BEATING EGG WHITES

For greatest volume, beat egg whites at room temperature in a clean, dry metal or glass bowl.

USING CHOCOLATE

Chocolate is best stored in a cool, dry place. Since it has a high content of cocoa butter, chocolate may develop a grey film, or "bloom," when temperatures change. This grey film does not affect the taste.

When melting chocolate, a low temperature is important to prevent overheating and scorching that will affect flavor and texture. The following are methods for melting chocolate:

- Chocolate can be melted in a heavy saucepan over low heat, stirring constantly until melted.

- Melting chocolate in a double boiler over hot, not boiling, water is a good method to prevent chocolate from overheating.

- Using a microwave to melt chocolate is fast and convenient. To microwave chocolate, place in a microwave-safe container and microwave on medium-high power (80%) 1 minute; stir with a dry spoon. Continue to microwave 15 seconds at a time, stirring chocolate after each interval until smooth. Frequent stirring is important, as the chocolate will appear not to be melting, but will be soft when stirred. A shiny appearance is another sign that chocolate is melting.

MAKING PATTERNS FOR COOKIES

Place a piece of white paper over pattern (for a more durable pattern, use acetate, a thin plastic used for stenciling that is available at craft stores). Use a permanent felt-tip pen with fine point to trace pattern; cut out pattern. Place pattern on rolled-out dough and use a small sharp knife to cut out cookies. (Note: If dough is sticky, dip knife frequently into flour while cutting out cookies.)

patterns

New Year's Toast Cookies
recipe on page 84, picture on page 85

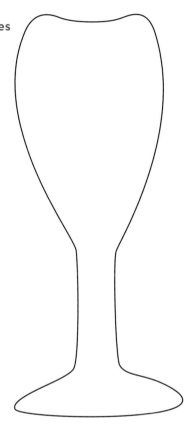

Sweetheart Meringues
recipe on page 87, picture on page 86

Carrot Cookies
*recipe on page 92,
picture on
page 93*

Nutty Neckties
*recipe on
page 96,
picture on page 97*

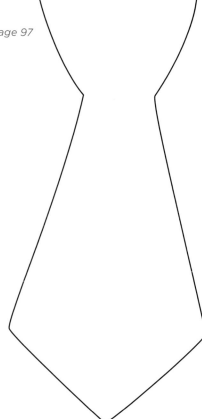

Flower Baskets
*recipe on page 95,
picture on page 94*

Fig. 1

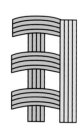

Fig. 2a

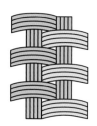

Fig. 2b

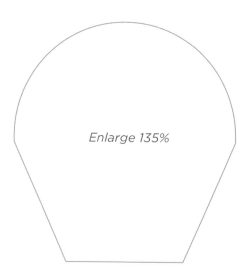

Enlarge 135%

metric equivalents

The recipes that appear in this cookbook use the standard United States method for measuring liquid and dry or solid ingredients (teaspoons, tablespoons, and cups). The information on this chart is provided to help cooks outside the U.S. successfully use these recipes. All equivalents are approximate.

METRIC EQUIVALENTS FOR DIFFERENT TYPES OF INGREDIENTS

A standard cup measure of a dry or solid ingredient will vary in weight depending on the type of ingredient. A standard cup of liquid is the same volume for any type of liquid. Use the following chart when converting standard cup measures to grams (weight) or milliliters (volume).

Standard Cup	Fine Powder (ex. flour)	Grain (ex. rice)	Granular (ex. sugar)	Liquid Solids (ex. butter)	Liquid (ex. milk)
1	140 g	150 g	190 g	200 g	240 ml
¾	105 g	113 g	143 g	150 g	180 ml
⅔	93 g	100 g	125 g	133 g	160 ml
½	70 g	75 g	95 g	100 g	120 ml
⅓	47 g	50 g	63 g	67 g	80 ml
¼	35 g	38 g	48 g	50 g	60 ml
⅛	18 g	19 g	24 g	25 g	30 ml

USEFUL EQUIVALENTS FOR LIQUID INGREDIENTS BY VOLUME

¼ tsp					=	1 ml	
½ tsp					=	2 ml	
1 tsp					=	5 ml	
3 tsp	=	1 tbls		½ fl oz	=	15 ml	
		2 tbls	=	⅛ cup	=	1 fl oz	=	30 ml
		4 tbls	=	¼ cup	=	2 fl oz	=	60 ml
		5 ⅓ tbls	=	⅓ cup	=	3 fl oz	=	80 ml
		8 tbls	=	½ cup	=	4 fl oz	=	120 ml
		10 ⅔ tbls	=	⅔ cup	=	5 fl oz	=	160 ml
		12 tbls	=	¾ cup	=	6 fl oz	=	180 ml
		16 tbls	=	1 cup	=	8 fl oz	=	240 ml
		1 pt	=	2 cups	=	16 fl oz	=	480 ml
		1 qt	=	4 cups	=	32 fl oz	=	960 ml
					=	33 fl oz	=	1000 ml	= 1 liter

USEFUL EQUIVALENTS FOR DRY INGREDIENTS BY WEIGHT
(To convert ounces to grams, multiply the number of ounces by 30.)

1 oz	=	¹⁄₁₆ lb	=	30 g
4 oz	=	¼ lb	=	120 g
8 oz	=	½ lb	=	240 g
12 oz	=	¾ lb	=	360 g
16 oz	=	1 lb	=	480 g

USEFUL EQUIVALENTS FOR LENGTH

(To convert inches to centimeters, multiply the number of inches by 2.5.)

1 in					= 2.5 cm	
6 in	=	½ ft			= 15 cm	
12 in	=	1 ft			= 30 cm	
36 in	=	3 ft	=	1 yd	= 90 cm	
40 in					= 100 cm	= 1 m

USEFUL EQUIVALENTS FOR COOKING/OVEN TEMPERATURES

	Fahrenheit	Celsius	Gas Mark
Freeze Water	32° F	0° C	
Room Temperature	68° F	20° C	
Boil Water	212° F	100° C	
Bake	325° F	160° C	3
	350° F	180° C	4
	375° F	190° C	5
	400° F	200° C	6
	425° F	220° C	7
	450° F	230° C	8
Broil			Grill

recipe index